EXCUSE US!

HERR SCHICKLGRUBER *
By H. Clifford Chadderton

A memoir of an officer who commanded an infantry company of the Royal Winnipeg Rifles (Canadian Army) in Normandy

* "Schicklgruber" was Hitler's birth name

D1091764

Layout: Diane Presley

Research: Verna Zadow

Production: Susan Trimble

ISBN 0-9735120-2-4
© The War Amputations of Canada
October 4, 2004

SPECIAL NOTE

Several publishers have expressed interest in bringing this Memoir to market as a commercial venture. The estimated price to a buyer, however, would be in the $35 range.

The intention in publishing the Memoir is that it will supplement the publications and documentaries produced by The War Amps under its Military Heritage program.

In order to achieve maximum distribution, therefore, we have been able to set a cost recovery price of $10, inclusive.

This was made possible through financial assistance from private sources.

This Memoir is in commemoration of the 60th anniversary of the end of World War II. It is a sincere tribute to those who served in the military forces and the Merchant Navy and to those who contributed to the tremendous work done on the 'HOMEFRONT.'

Canada has named 2005 as 'The Year Of The Veteran.'

Cliff Chadderton
Ottawa, Ontario
January 2005

Subsidized price $10.00 including postage and handling.
Signed copies by the author can be sent, with pleasure.

To facilitate enjoyment and understanding in this memoir:

- The narrative, which is in the form of individual stories (not necessarily in sequence), describes the author's experiences. It is in standard format; that is, "Here is your narrative."

- Diary entries are in a different type font. They were written immediately after the event. The type is like this.

- Excerpts from published material are again in different type – The type is like this.

- In some instances, stories of particular interest (but not in sequence) will appear. They are identified as Interlude

- Sidebars of significance are printed in 'box' form – usually shaded.

The chapters which follow have been written from my notes and the diary I carried with me throughout Normandy and Belgium. I stand behind the accuracy.

GEOGRAPHICAL NAMES

The second publication of the Manitoba Geographical Names Program entitled *A Place of Honour* took in many former Manitobans for whom an actual resting place could be found in the records of the Commonwealth War Graves Commission. The names in Manitoba cover lakes, islands, bays and other geographical fixtures. The book was published by the Manitoba Government in 2002 along with a topographical map which has an index. A number is given for grid scores from west to east and 11 squares identified by letter. Should a family wish to find and/or identify an actual geographical location, this can be done by following a road map issued by the Manitoba Government.

In this way, many Manitoba families have located the actual geographical feature. In some cases, it could also be found by locating the actual marker.

This will become much more clear when you read Chapter 44 entitled Odyssey. This Chapter describes my personal journey to find the feature for my Company Sergeant Major, BILLY BIRD.

The number of soldiers who went through the Royal Winnipeg Rifles during the eleven months of action was more than 1,800.

After demobilization, those that were still alive and whose disabilities allowed them to carry on life numbered approximately 1,350. On the other hand, we know that 450 others lay buried in graves in foreign soil. Concerning the wounded, the majority would be of a serious nature. This we know because a wound or injury of a lesser nature would be treated and the soldier would be sent back into action.

It is tremendous to realize that, in a small province like Manitoba, their 'place of honour' is commemorated in the geography of the province. This is explained in the following note to the book – *The Royal Winnipeg Rifles, In Recognition of Their Sacrifice, Commemorative Naming of Lakes, Islands, Bays and other Geographical Features.*

At the close of the Second World War, the Federal Government named a number of features across Canada after decorated Canadian casualties. This was often done without regard for the casualty's place of origin. Thus Manitoba has a number of features named after casualties who originated in other provinces and several Manitoba casualties are commemorated by a geographical feature outside Manitoba. In the interest of inclusiveness and wherever possible, all Royal Winnipeg Rifles casualties are included in 'A Place of Honour.' The lake, river or other feature named after these men and women is followed by an alphanumeric code throughout the body of the text (e.g., 64 G/15). This is the map reference in the National Topographic System (1:50,000 scale) on which this feature can be found. Reference to the map on the next page will give some indication of where the lake, hill, bay, etc., can be found.

MANITOBA GEOGRAPHIC MAP

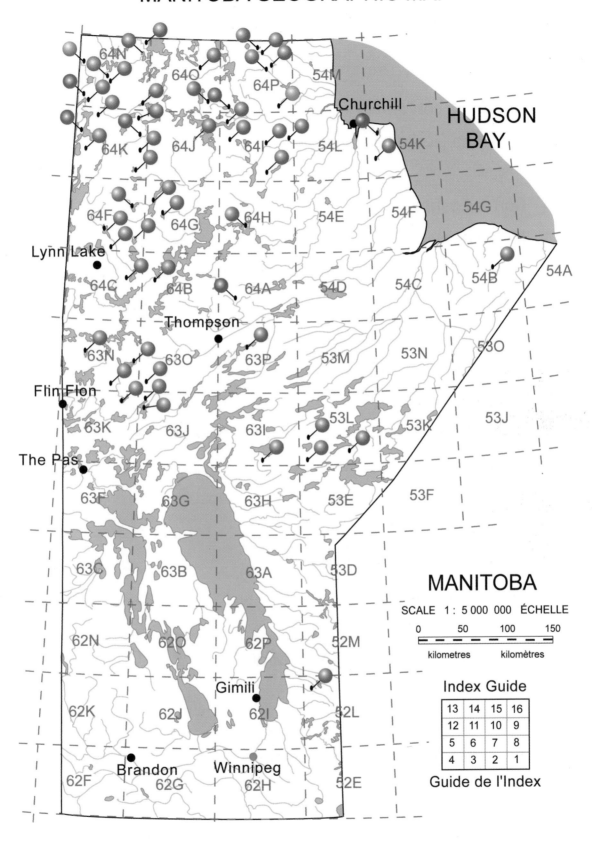

HUDSON BAY

64N
64O
64P
54M
Churchill
54L
54K
54G

64K
64J
64I
54F

64F
64G
64H
54E
54G

Lynn Lake
54B
54A

64C
64B
64A
54D
54C

Thompson

63N
63O
63P
53M
53N
53O

Flin Flon

63K
63J
63I
53L
53K
53J

The Pas

63F
63G
63H
53E
53F

63C
63B
63A
53D

62N
62O
62P
52M

Gimili
62K
62J
62I
52L

Brandon   Winnipeg
62F
62G
62H
52E

MANITOBA

SCALE 1 : 5 000 000 ÉCHELLE

0   50   100   150

kilometres   kilomètres

Index Guide

13	14	15	16
12	11	10	9
5	6	7	8
4	3	2	1

Guide de l'Index

TABLE OF CONTENTS

Chapter 1

BORROWED TIME

His home, his wife, and his child;
No thought had he for conquerors and kings,
Or reeking power and innocence defiled.

Then in an hour his soul was born again.

Robert J.C. Stead

A new lease on life! The world as I knew it was left behind, courtesy of the Armed Forces of **ADOLPH HITLER** (birth name - **SCHICKLGRUBER**). The time was approximately 10:00 hours Greenwich Mean Time (GMT) on October 10 '44. My new life commenced in the entrance to a bunker which had been built by the German SS defending that part of Holland which occupies the area from the Leopold Canal to the Scheldt Estuary and which runs into Antwerp from the North Sea. Part of a German defensive line was built on the North side of the Canal. A rough road ran from the bunker north towards Dutch towns such as Grafjan and Sluis in Holland.

My plans for a normal life (I was 25) ended in a fusillade of German artillery, helped by a German potato masher grenade dropped upon me by a leering German. My infantry company (down from 130 to 62 men due to shortage of reinforcements) occupied the remains of small bunkers on the German side of the raised canal bank.

Consciousness slowly came back. I realized that the guys I had soldiered with were feverishly digging me out.

I was alternating between excruciating pain and blissful peace which occurred when the mud compressed the wounds. I recall yelling for a stretcher-bearer. He came with morphine and pushed the needle into the only clean spot he could find – the crevice just above my collarbone. Wonderful relief as the analgesic flooded my veins! I closed my eyes. **SERGEANT ALEX BELL** – tall, fearless, tough – took charge. I could hear him shouting. He had found a small boat – actually a punt – large enough to ferry me back across the canal to where our medical staff were waiting at the Regimental Aid Post (RAP).

My next conscious moments might best be described as a hazy, almost boozy feeling. I was lying on a stretcher in the kitchen of a farm building. Our regimental medical officer – the much admired **DOC CALDWELL** from Yarmouth, Nova Scotia – was trying to revive me. He said to his medical orderlies "Don't let him suffer." A bad omen?

DOC CALDWELL asked **GEORGE HAYWOOD**, one of his assistants, if he had gone through my personal effects. I was married and my wife was in Winnipeg. They were looking for incriminating letters, maybe written to a girl in England where I had spent four years. This was standard procedure.

GEORGE'S reply came through to me, despite my semi-conscious state: "Not this guy. I don't think the Piccadilly commandos interested him; anyway, he devoted all his time to sports." They told me later I laughed.

Next stop: The Casualty Clearing Station (CCS), where they applied tourniquets and gave me another shot of morphine. At the same time, they attempted to treat a serious wound in the stomach which could prove fatal if peritonitis set in. **DOC CALDWELL** had undoubtedly saved my life. He had identified the stomach wound back at the Regimental Aid Post (RAP) and stuffed it with sulpha powder. As he was performing this procedure, he said the words which would be with me for the rest of my life. He was talking to **ERNIE PASH** – another much-respected medic: "From now on **CLIFF CHADDERTON** is LIVING ON BORROWED TIME."

My next lucid moment came as I lay in a corridor of a building turned into a hospital. This was the third step in the evacuation – first the RAP; then the CCS; and at last the Canadian General Field Hospital (CGFH). We were in the Belgian town of Eecloo. The effects of the morphine were still with me. A doctor, performing triage, stripped away the blood-stained parts of my battledress. Walking wounded lined the corridor. The battlefield surgeon told them they would have to wait until he tended to this officer (me) whose wounds he classified as 'probably fatal.' The expression set off a jolt in the pit of my stomach – then my thought was 'what the heck, that Jerry bombardment could have killed me in any event.'

Eventually orderlies carried me inside the resuscitation ward. Waxing and waning between life and death is recalled (not to put too fine a dramatic spin on it).

Later, a doctor examined me. He said mine was the last surgery he could handle that day. It was midnight. My mood brightened when the duty nurse repeated to me the surgeon's words "This may be your lucky day!"

I remember snatches of those hours: the blood-stained gurney; the fact that my shoes were gone; the anaesthetic needles; the dissipation of the pain when it reached an unbearable degree; and the nagging question – 'what had happened to my men?'

A vague debate trickled through my sub-conscious mind. Would they take off my right leg or my left leg? The doctor told the nurse: "I think I can save one." The nurse kept finding new shrapnel wounds, 13 in all.

My next memory was of lying in a gymnasium. The surgery was over. The floor was choc-a-bloc with stretchers holding the wounded, earmarked to go to England via a DC-3. The RCAF 'Workhorse' aircraft was doing duty as an ambulance plane. Gratefully, another shot of morphine, and I was lying on a make-shift bed in the plane. One semi-conscious sergeant across the aisle from me was mumbling: "I came all the way from D-Day to Holland without a scratch. Now they're sending me back to the U.K. I hope my luck holds because this aircraft looks to be a pretty good target." Bright thought, that!

YOU'LL NEVER HEAR THE ONE THAT GETS YOU...

The old 'sweats' who had already been through a war were fond of saying, as a new boy would cock his ear and listen for an incoming shell, 'Don't worry lad, you'll never hear the one that gets you.'

No truer words were spoken. When the shell came, it was quick ... I heard nothing!

Chapter 2

MEDEVAC

Reality is merely an illusion, albeit a very persistent one.

Albert Einstein

Most who sustain serious wounds relive the experience in dreams. The author is no exception.

Usually, in the dream sequence, a type of consciousness takes hold. It would feel as if the guys with whom I had soldiered were digging me out. Morphine interferes with the brain. The incidents kept coming back in snatches – shatteringly realistic – so realistic it sometimes took (takes) hours to convince myself that I had been dreaming. A typical dream sequence would see me, in my wandering mind, alternating between excruciating pain and blissful peace. During one of my more lucid moments, I would yell for a stretcher-bearer, who would come with morphine. Blessed relief as the analgesic flooded my veins (in my dreams).

These hallucinations continued for years. In fact, I still wrestle with 'the beast' now and again ... 60 years later.

Another part of the dream – a growing apprehension. As a duck hunter, flat-bottomed punts were a favourite mode of transportation. At the level of the floor boards it was normal to find inches of water. This particular homemade boat had a dry bottom. Gradually, though, in my dream, it began to fill with blood. Terrifying! **ALEX BELL** was going to make certain that I got across the canal, but was fumbling with a field dressing which consisted of a lump of gauze and about two and a half feet of bandage. He was having a hell of a time. I told him to stem the artery in the side of my right thigh with a tourniquet. It was one of those instances where scraps of lectures, heard in a hut back in Camp Shilo, came through. I remember telling him how to bind the artery which, with his big sure farmer's hands, he could do. The tourniquet cut off the artery and the spurts of blood stopped. It saved my life.

Here the dream dissolves. Was it real? Did it happen this way? Real or imagined?

I do remember at the time uttering words of thanks to an absent **Sgt. Alex Montgomery**, our first-aid instructor at an army camp years ago. Thanks to the good old-fashioned twist of a strung-out field dressing, using a piece of wood as a handle, the geysers of blood which were reaching two feet, were properly staunched.

The most prophetic words in the dream were those of **Doc Caldwell**. They will remain with me for the rest of my life. They are worth repeating. "BORROWED TIME!" The dream usually ends here.

Al Jardine played a role in my MEDEVAC phase. If this reaches him, I take it all back. We went through officers' training school together. He was criticized because he made no bones about his plans - - he would get a desk job rather than take a posting to the infantry.

By coincidence, **Al Jardine** was in the triage room at Bramshott Military Hospital? He pulled down the blanket which someone had placed over my head, an indication that I was a 'goner.' Excitedly he shouted for an orderly. "I know this guy! Why the hell is he going to the morgue? He's still alive!"

In the shuffle on the air ambulance, I had been tagged 'Dead.' **Al Jardine** realized that I was seriously wounded but not yet ready for the Graves Registration Unit. **Al** took it upon himself to push me to the emergency ward, where they plied me with plasma. I was shortly on my way to some kind of recovery.

I thanked **Al Jardine** several days later. He said, jokingly, that he was only paying me back for the fruit I had stolen from his father's horse and buggy. The elder **Jardine** was well known to us kids in Fort Rouge in Winnipeg. When **Al's** father came down the road with his wagon of fresh fruit, we took the opportunity to relieve him of a few watermelons or whatever choice fruit he was peddling that day.

Chapter 3

MOBILIZATION AND

THE FIRST REGIMENTAL SERGEANT MAJOR (RSM)

Well may the world read a lesson, well may it learn, and be wise;
Not to the strong is the battle; not to the swift is the prize;
Loud is the boast of the despot, clanking his nations in arms,
But beware of a peace-loving people
when they sweep from their forests and farms.

Robert J.C. Stead

The Royal Winnipeg Rifles (RWR) mobilized in June '40 - - the month that **HITLER** occupied the Lowlands.

As a general rule, ordinary soldiers viewed Regimental Sergeant Majors (RSMs) with respect – but with a great deal of caution. Junior officers regarded them either as an incarnation of evil or a real friend who could show them the ropes.

Presumably, Ottawa thought it was high time to activate one of the famous infantry regiments – preferably one with some history. The existence of the RWR, better known as the Little Black Devils, goes back to the Riel Rebellion of 1885. That is when the Regiment acquired the name. When the Winnipeg Rifles attacked the Métis, their leaders, who had been battling with the red-coated Royal Northwest Mounted Police, were supposed to have exclaimed: "We know those Redcoats, but who are those Little Black Devils?" (Rifle Regiments wear black hats and webbing.)

The first full World War II parade of the Regiment was in July '40. The RSM was **LEN SMITH,** a WWI veteran. He had been the Chief of Police of Winnipeg – a tall, broad, commanding figure.

Want to know a little about him? This is an actual event I witnessed while covering the Police beat as a reporter. One summer night in 1939, a telephone call informed us that the infamous Atamonchuk brothers (Mike the Horse, and Joe) were holed up in a house in North Winnipeg. Three months earlier they had murdered two clerks in the offices of the Manitoba Motor League – the loot was a paltry forty dollars.

SMITTY (the name Len preferred when talking off the record with the media) called on the Atamonchuks to surrender. Joe asked for clemency. **SMITTY** swore that, if Joe came out shooting, he would leave in a hearse – and he did! Brother Mike surrendered. He was hanged in the old City Jail in Winnipeg. The media was there.

A good many recruits shared the thought 'how could we lose a war with **SMITTY** as the RSM?' His real value was symbolic to young soldiers.

To 'his boys,' his introduction was in a football field across from the headquarters of the Hudson's Bay Company on Main Street in Winnipeg. His criticisms to young soldiers were in gentlemanly tones. He walked up and down, then mounted a chair. In a quiet voice, he mumbled: "I've seen worse troops" – pregnant pause – then added as his voice rose, "<u>But not much</u>!"

The battalion needed **SMITTY** to whip it into parade ground shape. Age caught up with him. He went as far as England and was posted to administrative duties.

Chapter 4

CAREER PATH

People forget how fast you did a job –
but they remember how well you did it.

Howard Newton

My career path after High School was a jumble – University to study law …
working shifts as a Reporter. Bottom line though was to play hockey for the
New York Rangers. My Junior 'A' hockey was with the Ranger's Farm Club
in Winnipeg.   The calibre of that league was, as sports writers say, of a
standard that would qualify the player for a spot in the NHL of today.

I attended training camp in Winnipeg for the Rangers in 1939. My father
had signed the necessary 'C' form with the organization. The nod from
coach Frank Boucher, and I played two exhibition games with the Rangers.
War was coming, however, and I had a Lieutenant commission with The
Rifles. The Regiment had always had a very good hockey team. In fact,
the RWR (Little Black Devils) won the Manitoba senior championship in
1939, back when the Senior league was something with which to be
reckoned.

In June '40 the hockey stick was traded for a rifle. I joined as a private
soldier, thinking the war would be over by Christmas; also, that I had no
real qualifications to lead troops as an officer. (Later in the war, I did get
my commission.)

The RWR moved to Camp Shilo in South West Manitoba. I kept up my
obligation with the Rangers and when we moved to Camp Debert in Nova
Scotia, I played in the Maritime Senior Hockey League against such
aggregations as the Moncton Hawks, the Glace Bay Miners and the Truro
Bear Cats. It was in the latter part of the 1940-41 season.

But, back to my story line.

Chapter 5

CAMP SHILO, MANITOBA

Necessity is the plea for every infringement of human freedom.
It is the argument of tyrants; it is the creed of slaves.

William Pitt

Our first training centre was Camp Shilo located between Winnipeg and Brandon, Manitoba. Here there was some 'comic relief.'

Brandon, 20 miles west of Shilo, was the nearest town with any nightlife. It was a bone-shattering 40-minute ride, courtesy of the 'Ledoux Express' – an assortment of jalopies owned by two brothers – members of the RWR, who were experts at operating vehicles of questionable reliability. The charge was twenty-five cents. The convoy left for Brandon every afternoon.

Returning to camp was different. The army furnished vehicles which left when the drivers decided it was time.   Riding shotgun with the drivers would be a military policeman – not always good company. The unfortunate late-comers walked back to camp. They appeared worse for wear on parade the next day.

They were known as the 'Shilo-shufflers'. They sang or whistled an old drinking song, as follows:

> *Show me the way to go home,*
> *I'm tired and I want to go to bed,*
> *I had a little drink about an hour ago,*
> *And it's gone right to my head.*

They were required to take 'one step' forward. The late returnees found themselves on latrine duty.

Going into Winnipeg – some 140 miles east – was a different proposition. The train stopped at Douglas, about five miles north of the camp. Friendly locomotive engineers, most of whom had been in the trenches in World War I, made an unscheduled stop to pick up the Winnipeg-bound soldiers lined up along the 'right of way.' The trains ran on a schedule more reliable than the 'Ledoux Express!' A huge understatement!

One incident will always remain with some of us – literally. A big American soldier by the name of **EARL WEATHERALL** had joined the Regiment – naturally we called him 'Yank.' He fancied himself as somewhat of an artist with India ink and a needle. Soldiers arriving back late at night were often wrestled to the floor, pinned down, and tattooed. They were seldom given the luxury of choice. Imagine these soldiers, some barely eighteen years of age, arriving home on their next leave with startling permanent tattoos such as 'Death Before Dishonour,' decorating the deltoid muscle! My tattoo is the nickname of my first wife. A sailing ship disguising the name DOT. She died some twenty years ago. I said the incident would remain with some of us literally. Mine is still visible.

The training in Shilo was parade ground … spit and polish for shoes, blanco for webbing, brasso for buttons. We complained that the army invention called 'square bashing' on the hard cement was unsuitable preparation for the blitzkrieg soldiers of the Third Reich. We took note of the goose-stepping Nazis from the news reels in the theatres.

It was a relief to hear that the Regiment was heading for the East coast of Canada and then across the Atlantic. The train coaches had wooden benches. Food was prepared days ahead – usually haversack lunches, i.e., 20 sandwiches per cardboard box. The RWR were going to war. Disgust filled the air when the train stopped at a place called Debert in Nova Scotia. The Camp was still under construction. Tar paper and green lumber is remembered. This was to be our home until the call to embark for England.

Chapter 6

CAMP DEBERT, N,S.

Nothing is a waste of time if you use the experience wisely.

Rodin

A large number of Canadian soldiers who ended up in combat went through the staging camp at Debert. I would like to say: "Training for War is Hell" – to quote U.S. General William T. Sherman of the U.S. Civil War. That applied in Debert, but there were lighter moments.

It was winter. We had pot-bellied stoves in the centre of the wooden huts. The windowpanes were portable but there were only enough for one side. Hence, we had to move our beds from side to side to protect ourselves from the cold rain or snow.

Debert was to test our mettle. Most of the RWRs had seen tough times in civilian life, but at least would have had a bed, toilet facilities, sports equipment and a way to enjoy life, the 'great depression' notwithstanding. The environment of the army changed all that. Debert was a sparse land, reputed to have been sold to the Government by some astute politician at an inflated cost. Looking back now, those who experienced it would recall a regimented life, most of it lived in drafty H Huts, the parade square or route marches along the sometimes dismal roads in that part of otherwise picturesque Nova Scotia. The harvester helpers from the West, the fishermen, the trappers, the mechanics, and the inner-city dwellers would have an average age of late teens or early twenties. An army was a great place to develop friendships but there were few perks. Debert will long-live in the memory of those who went through it and survived the war.

A sad tale to usher in the RWR arrival ... FIDO (WILLIAM) PURPER was one of the first casualties of the Regiment. He was on a live training exercise. Bullets were to be jammed with wadding, but the rifle that got FIDO was loaded with a genuine .303 lead bullet. It penetrated his chest. He died shortly after. The entire battalion lined the station platform. The bugle sounded the Last Post. It would not be the last time we stood motionless, listening to those mournful notes. We watched as the West bound train departed, carrying his body back to Manitoba. His geographical marker is *Purper Lake* (52 L/11)[*] in Manitoba.

Another incident, this one with a funny twist, has gone down in the annals of the Little Black Devils. One day the RSM was unable to show up to give the order for the nightly two-and-a-half mile run. **LT BRIAN LAVER** had joined the Rifles from university ranks. To the troops he was a bit of an ass. He was told to take over the RSM's function. As he gave the order: "Rifles, commence your run," one of his sergeant platoon commanders said, "How will we know when to come back?" Our wimpy subaltern (army lingo for lieutenant), who went to a staff job before D-Day, said, "When I make a noise like a buffalo, you will all return to me in the middle of the parade ground."

He should have known better than to give an order of this kind to the guys who made up the RWR. On **LAVER'S** orders we ran to the middle of a heavy copse. Suddenly we heard a sound, something like 'Woo-ah!' Laver's Buffalo belch?

The boys of the Rifles turned to each other. Their collective thought was: 'Which way is Truro?' None admitted knowing the sound a buffalo makes. A night on the town beckoned. It was easy to thumb a ride on a vehicle going to Truro. Some of the more adventurous even went to Bible Hill - - but more information on this destination won't be in this memoir. The usual bellow was 'Get off the table, Mabel, the two bucks is for the beer.'

Some swear by the rest of the **LAVER** story – that is, this particular Lieutenant continued for hours, making a noise which he insisted was that of a buffalo, probably in heat! No RWRs returned to him.

A third incident from Debert days – either very funny or tragic, depending on your point of view. A traveling circus was in Truro. An altercation took place between one of the roustabouts (the tough guys who work around circuses) and a member of one of the Canadian units. A pistol shot from a roustabout – and a Canadian soldier lay dead.

---

[*] Throughout this Memoir we have used alphanumeric codes to signify the location of a lake, river or other feature named after these men. A further explanation can be found on page iii. The Manitoba Geographic Map is found on page v.

Next day, the Brigade Commander, **Brig W.K. 'Shorty' Colquhoun**, confined the entire camp to barracks until further notice.

Not a popular move! The word went around. That evening there would be an impromptu gathering on a hill overlooking the circus. H-Hour was when darkness fell. On a given command (there was never a better organized attack), the Canadians would charge. As the mighty swarm swept down the hill, a battle cry evolved. It was not mean-spirited and an indication that the troops never really intended to do anything serious. Anyway, the battle cry was a time-worn circus chant:

> Ice cream, ice cream
>
> Freeze your tongue and give your teeth a sleigh ride.

Prior orders given by the troops themselves said no circus people were to be fatal casualties. This did not include the plastic horses from the merry-go-round and various other pieces of equipment owned by the circus. The fighting troops of the brigade levelled the equipment, sideshows and all.

I was sleeping off-base in a house in Truro. Next morning my trusty bicycle was carrying me to catch the regimental bus back to camp. I could scarcely believe my eyes. The streets of Truro were littered with broken heads of fake circus ponies, whirligig chairs – you name it.

It would depend on your point of view. Was this a story with a happy ending, or otherwise. Under the power vested in him as Commander, **Shorty Colquhoun** levied damages against every man-jack in the brigade. All were willing to pay. At least they had something exciting about which to write home.

Regimental histories allude to 'the circus' as their first combat action.

Jack Mitchell: The tale of Debert had another humorous incident - one afternoon, given over to R&R, saw the conversation turn to how we might handle fear. My sidekick, **Jack Mitchell**, was looking at a very high water tower. He challenged anyone to climb the flimsy outside steps and give the victory sign from the very peak. My pal (?) volunteered my services. There was a ledge around the top which required the climber to grab onto a metal gutter and swing his legs over to the roof. A fall would be 100 feet to

Mother Earth and probably 'curtains.' I somehow made it. Then Jack did the same.

It had not occurred to us that coming down would be more hazardous. It meant scrabbling down a sloping roof, grabbing the steel gutter and swinging our legs underneath, being sure to make contact with the rungs of the makeshift ladder which was at least three feet under the roof's edge. I was first. The escapade nearly killed me. I slipped but grabbed the fourth rung from the top just in time.

Next was **JACK**. To the jeers of a gathering crowd, it took **JACK** three tries but he survived the ordeal. This guy knew no fear as his actions, once we hit the beach in Normandy, proved.

Jack Mitchell and Cliff Chadderton - - Debert 1940

THE TRURO BEAR CATS: It would be criminal to complete the story of the RWR in Debert without telling one more comical episode. The Truro Bear Cats were playing the Moncton Hawks. One of the referees was a little one-sided, to put it mildly.

After some atrocious calls in favour of Moncton, The Truro star defenceman, **FRASER EADIE** (later Commanding Officer of the 1st Canadian Parachute Regiment) complained to league officials.

The verbal exchange was overheard by **RFN PHILIP ZASTRE** – one of the genuine characters of the unit who was killed on June 6 '44.

ZASTRE came down to the end of the rink where the wives of the Truro players were given standing room only (SRO). One of the referees did not show up. As a result, a player from the Moncton Hawks, who was injured but could still skate, was dragooned into wearing a striped jersey.

ZASTRE, with a little astute detective work, found out that the Moncton player (referee) had a bad back. He had come from Moncton ready to play and was wearing his wife's girdle for support.

During the intermission, HARTLEY WEATHERBY, who lived nearby and was the Truro team manager, told his wife the story. She spread the word among the other wives. They rushed out and brought back some unmentionables of various sizes.

When play resumed, the first questionable call by our Moncton Hawk referee was greeted with a clothesline of girdles, garter belts and other women's accoutrement. Word spread that the referee, who was giving the Truro Bear Cats a lot of trouble, was wearing his wife's girdle.

He lasted two more one-sided calls. The bogus referee was literally laughed off the ice.

The actual score of the game is lost in the mists of time. The wives of the Truro Bear Cats had earned at least an assist on some goals.

This next part of the story might come under the heading of 'apocryphal.' It happened two years later. It was told on good authority, however, that, on his jump to get ready for D-Day, someone stuffed a girdle in FRASER EADIE'S pouch which he had tied to his pack. He broke his leg on the jump and was unable to make the airborne assault into France. Whether the girdle had anything to do with it – well, who knows? Fraser saw plenty of war in later jumps into enemy territory.

Lt. Gen. Ernie Sansom

We did some training but we still had wooden rifles. There was, however, one genuine Lee Enfield .303. On a certain day, **Gen E.W. (Ernie) Sansom** was to visit the firing range. The officer in charge told all of the troops in the butts (pits) except number five to hold down their targets. **Sansom** appeared on the firing point with a great entourage. He said, "I will put six bulls eyes in target number six." Now, the officer in charge had pre-placed the bullet holes in target number five. Target number six, of course, remained untouched. The good general fired off a clip. The order was given asking the target marker on number six to run up with the target. He did so. There were no hits.

The officer in charge probably went a long way in the army. He said, to all assembled: "Gentlemen, we thought we would play a little joke on the general. We had him firing blanks!"

To show that he had recognized the prank, **Ernie** said that it reminded him of the story of the village idiot who could put a bullet in the centre of any target. Asked how he did it he said: "Simple – you shoot the bullet first and then draw the bullseye afterwards."

Chapter 7

OVERSEAS (AT LAST)

CANADIAN ARMY WAITS UNTIL HITLER SHARPENS HIS SWORD
Headline from Winnipeg Tribune

January 2, 1942 – "Canadian Army -- a dagger pointed at the heart of Berlin."

Quoted from statement of
Lt. Gen. Andy McNaughton
Commander, Canadian Forces in Europe

The SS Orbita, a banana boat in pre-war parlance, took our Regiment across the submarine-infested North Atlantic in 1941. A never-to-be forgotten picture, etched in my mind, was when the boat was leaving the dock in Halifax. Wives and sweethearts were standing, waving. The rifle contingent was standing to at the starboard railing of the stout old vessel. Many were singing the song made popular by Abbey Cook, an RWR from Selkirk, Manitoba. The words are well-remembered.

> "Put me in your pocket
> So that I'll be close to you
> No more will I be lonely and
> No more will I be blue
> And when it comes to parting
> There'll be no sad adieu
> Cause I'll be in your pocket
> And I'll go along with you"

The rest of '41 and all of '42, was spent engaged in the defence of Britain, occupying positions in the dangerous South Coast of England. We could be called out on the command 'Pickets Blue' to defend against the possible invasion by the forces of **ADOLF HITLER**.

Our military unit continued in this defensive role, at the same time engaging in high-level training to carry out any cross-channel attack.

We were trained to the hilt by the time we landed in Britain, but our weapons were pitiful. The only defence against the 45-ton tank was the Boys rifle, which fired a 45mm single shot. Some joke!

This was the situation up until the 3rd Canadian Division was called to be part of the assault on the 'Festung Europa' defensive fortifications – known today as D-Day.

The discrepancies between the German and the Canadian small arms left much to be desired.

COMPARISON TABLE		
	GERMAN	CANADIAN
SIDEARM	Lugers and the P 38 – (a cheaper copy of the Luger)	.38 calibre Revolvers (World War I version)
RIFLES	Mauser	Brit .303 (World War I version)
Machine Guns (fixed)	Spandau (600 rpm)	Bren (500 rpm)
Machine Guns (hand held)	Schmeisser (500 rpm)	Sten (totally unreliable)

It was a stimulating time to be in the Armed Forces. Notwithstanding the table above, it is interesting to look at our personal weapons. They included sheath knives, Sten guns, .303 rifles with bayonets, and grenades. We had no effective large weapons available to oppose a German invasion. The impression of the troops was that we were commandos – ready to attack – not to defend. It was helpful in creating 'fighting spirit' – and it did! Once it was known that the RWR was scheduled to play a leading role in the invasion of Europe (Juno Beach), the training was rough with plenty of rugged 'schemes' with names like SPARTAN and Exercise TIGER. No one complained.

We knew what we would be facing. The German Army was probably the best in the world.

Chapter 8

A COURAGEOUS SUBALTERN
ROD BEATTIE

Courage is resistance to fear, mastery of fear - not absence of fear.

Mark Twain

This is a tragic tale which stretches more than 40 years. It is best to start in a light-hearted manner.

Back in the early days of the war, battalion orders were preceded by bugle calls.

The regimental bugler would mount the steps and blow the 'fall-in.'

This did not rank as the most welcome bugle call. Its popularity was superseded by the famous mail call which went:

Speaking of buglers, we had a Company Sergeant Major (CSM) by the name of **ALF SAVAGE**. On an evening pass to Truro, N.S., **ALF** got into a tremendous fight with some senior NCOs from another regiment. Our CO's punishment for **ALF** – he was 'broken' from CSM to Assistant Regimental Bugler and put on the wagon. One famous day in Debert Camp, the RSM paraded **ALF SAVAGE** before the Battalion and asked him how he was doing in his new job. He replied that he had downed so many different kinds of pop he was urinating rainbows. So much for **ALF SAVAGE**.

One mail call will always be remembered. It was about May 15 '44. D-Day was getting close. The Winnipegs were sealed in camps, surrounded by 10-foot canvas fencing. These were the staging areas for the troops who would carry out the D-Day assault.

The mail call went out. A few young officers were lounging near **ROD BEATTIE'S** tent. **ROD**, a newly-minted subaltern, had been raised on Walker Avenue, in the Fort Rouge district of Winnipeg.

The mail corporal threw a package into our bivouac tent. It was addressed to **ROD** and there was a note from Pop – the familiar name by which **ROD'S** dad was known. It was a box of fudge. **ROD** and his buddies gathered around to devour the contents.

Pop Beattie worked at the Manitoba Wheat Pool. He had one of the chemists make up some fudge which contained 'crystallized alcohol.'

The results were hilarious. Four officers of the Rifles were sprawled around enjoying the odd-tasting candy. The stories got wilder by the minute, as they devoured most of the contents. Then the effect began to take its toll. Score: 'Pop' Beattie – 4; RWR Officers – 0.

There was a sequel. **LT. COL. JOHN MELDRAM** – our CO – had a sense of humour. When the RSM paraded four hung-over young subalterns before him, the CO took one look and asked for a piece of the fudge. He pretended not to like it… but we were left to wonder. His batman said he was ill that evening. Something he ate?

ROD BEATTIE landed on D-Day with Baker Company. He took a machine gun bullet to the spine. In an act which goes beyond bravery, his Company **CSM BILLY WALSH** – known throughout Canada as a Dominion Brier curling champion – reached back and dragged **ROD** ashore.

ROD ended up in a ward in Deer Lodge Hospital in Winnipeg. A very specific job had to be done. **ROD** was 'down in the dumps.' No wonder – he was paralyzed from the waist down. When I arrived back in Winnipeg in December '44, the medics thought that I, as an old friend, could perhaps boost his sagging morale. We were given a double room!

ROD could not lift himself. We brought in a plumber who rigged up some piping swiped from a pile of building material. The contraption he devised had a handle and a chain. It allowed **ROD** to hoist himself up.

One of the better stories of our hospital stay involved a wonderful nurse by the name of **ALICE**.[*]

ROD was concerned and wondered whether, being a paraplegic, he would be able to perform his manly duties. He was being visited regularly by an attractive girl named **EDIE**.

We developed a 'test' with the co-operative **NURSE ALICE**. She was a willing accomplice. After lights out on a particular evening, an orderly wheeled my bed out of our room. **ALICE** came in. She was just off duty. She looked ravishing.

ROD was not 'in' on the deal. **ALICE** had agreed to make a few sensual passes at **ROD**, as he lay in his hospital bed.

She said: "If I can't find out what **ROD** wants to know, I will be very surprised – so will my boyfriend!"

The music was right, the time was right. The experiment, however, was a dismal failure. **ALICE** came out in tears, shaking her head. They wheeled me back in and I looked at **ROD**. He was roaring with laughter. It would take more than his hopes for an erection (or lack thereof) to quell his spirit. We had a hidden bottle of Chianti wine and celebrated most of the night away. When **ALICE** came on duty the next evening, she was equal to the task of telling **ROD** that there were 'other ways.' **ROD** was born of a generation, however, that only knew of 'one way' so that was it.

---

[*] Name has been changed.

The next evening, **ROD'S** lady friend came in and it was left to me to tell her the story. She suggested adoption as an option. In fact that did take place. **ROD** and **EDIE** got married and adopted two wonderful girls.

There is no requirement to flesh out the tragic parts of this. Suffice it to say that no one wants to live the life of a paraplegic. Confined to a bed or wheelchair, bed sores, forced enemas, unsatisfied desires. The only saving grace was **ROD'S** good humour. We often got a chuckle out of the reminiscences of our training days – and of course the story of the 'fudge' sent to him by Pop Beattie – to say nothing of **ALICE**.

Digging a little deeper into the **ROD BEATTIE** story, there is interesting material. In Kelvin High School, **ROD** was a straight 'A' student. Not that he didn't play sports, but with a brain like his, it would have been a sheer waste if he didn't go to university. **ROD** was 21 years of age when he led his platoon against the huge concrete emplacement at the junction of the Seulles River and the English Channel, i.e., Juno Beach.

What does a war cost in human terms? The example of **ROD BEATTIE** is worth some thought. He was cut down by a German machine gunner in the prime of life. The 40 years he managed to exist (and it was an existence the hell of which no one could possibly conceive) were made liveable only by the sacrifices of his wonderful wife and adoring daughters ... and the help of his friends, mostly ex-RWR.

ROD could have pursued a university degree after the war but the constant pain and struggle of his life made this impossible. Most of those 40 years was spent in difficult jobs. He did, however, operate the first electronic dictating system in the Manitoba Legislature. A great opportunity? Not if your after-work life is pure hell. Pain, constant experimentation with callipers (leg irons) to see if he could get some mobility, dependence upon his wife and daughters for transportation (no joke in a Manitoba winter).

Despite the pain and frustration, **ROD** found the time, along with another RWR paraplegic by the name of **TONY MANN**, to found the Manitoba Branch of the Canadian Paraplegic Association – an organization which was the springboard leading to a series of paraplegic hospitals across Canada. These institutions assist not only war veterans, but paraplegics in general.

I recall hooking up with him in Toronto at a meeting of the Canadian Paraplegic Association. One evening we headed for the seamy part of town to have a little fun. ROD, on such occasions, had to strap a rubber urinal over his waterworks. The portable rubber urinal – as it was called – strung down the side of ROD'S hospital pants and could be accessed through an inside zipper from his crotch to below his knee.

After a few Boilermakers (a favourite Western Canadian concoction – cheap rye whisky and draft beer), ROD needed a 'facility.' We wheeled him into a darkened corner in the bar. ROD had to carry a flashlight so that he could operate his urinal. He unzipped his trouser leg and out popped a long 14-inch container which looked like an oversized condom. Just then, two girls came out of the dark. At the crucial moment, the flashlight showed what looked like a very huge part of the male anatomy. The girls laughed and brought back several of their cohorts of the night with them. They told us that they would be assured of free beers for the rest of the evening if they could tell ROD'S story. The rest is left to the imagination!

I telephoned ROD in 1984 when a buddy said he was very low. I was living in Ottawa; he was in Winnipeg. I tried to pep him up a bit with some stories. ROD'S wry humour came through, but he ended up by saying "Nice try, old buddy, but don't feel sorry for me. I am ready to go." He died the next week.

When I commenced this memoir, a promise passed through my mind. I could not avoid tragic incidents but would try to find the brighter side. ROD BEATTIE'S story provided at least some great examples.

Chapter 9

TONY THE ITALIAN

*The meeting of two personalities is like
the contact of two chemical substances:
if there is any reaction, both are transformed.*

Carl Jung

Back to England. **TONY** had quite a war. He was conscripted into the Italian Army. By an odd coincidence, we became friends.

TONY fought against the British in North Africa. He was taken prisoner by an English Major and sent to a Prisoner of War (POW) compound in Shropshire, England, near the border of Wales.

Like many 'tame' Italian POWs, he was loaned out to a farmer in Britain to help with the crops. He had given his solemn word that he would not escape. It so happened that he was being employed by **DUDLEY HESKETH**, my father's cousin.

On my first visit to **DUDLEY**, **TONY** (I never knew his real name) proudly showed me the sleeping quarters which had been fixed up for him in a barn. It was impressive to see how comfortable he had made himself – borrowing pictures to hang; even poems ripped out from magazines were on the wall. Also, he spent considerable time learning English. He was a classical scholar.

TONY became part of Dudley's family. He joined us at meals and the discussions after the table was cleared were fascinating. He told us quite a bit about the Italian Army, including the knowledge that they were badly misled by **MUSSOLINI**, who had been quite willing to loan his entire army to **ADOLF HITLER'S** plans of world conquest.

TONY was great company. **DUDLEY** was in the English Home Guard. This particular unit had a lot of fun. They did not take the army too seriously, although they would have fought to the last man if necessary. **DUDLEY** asked me to go to a training session ... a bayonet skills session ... on how a sergeant in the Canadian Army could skewer Germans who did not want to give up the fight. **TONY** came along by mutual agreement. The plan was that he would be the enemy and we would put on a real demonstration in the pub where the Home Guard congregated. Wooden rifles were the order of the day, of course, and the entire episode was enjoyed by the local pub crawlers.

On one unforgettable evening, **TONY** presented me with a .410 shotgun. I never asked where he got it. **UNCLE DUDLEY** joined us for rabbit hunts on a number of occasions. This might sound like a cruel sport. Anyone who believes that has never been on a rabbit hunt. The rabbits (or hares) could move very quickly. It took a pretty good shot to knock them down. Some people may be a bit squeamish if they knew that we took the rabbits home and **DUDLEY'S** wife would cook up a meal of rabbit stew. Delicious!

When I returned from leave, I tried to tell some of my buddies about **TONY**. It was only when I could get some photos that there was some semblance of belief.

Toward the end of 1943, the Italian Army surrendered. POWs like **TONY** were no longer legally Prisoners of War. The British were rather short of a certain type of soldier. To be polite, we will give them the term 'batmen' but they were known throughout the British Army as 'manservants.'

The CO of the British Army unit which had taken **TONY** prisoner kept in touch with him while he was at **DUDLEY'S** farm. When the British Army began taking in the former POWs who had been in the Italian Forces, this enterprising Major came armed with the necessary papers. Would **TONY** enlist in the Major's battalion? **TONY**, whose sympathies had never been with either the Italians or the Germans and who had grown to like the English very much, was quick to nod in the affirmative. Dudley wrote to tell me that **TONY** joined the British Army. His unit was being groomed as part of a British Division, and would in all likelihood be fighting in Europe.

During the hours which we spent around **UNCLE DUDLEY**'s fireplace, **TONY**, who had mastered English to the point where we could easily converse, told us about his boyhood. He had been raised in the Cesena area in the north of Italy. He was a crack shot with a rabbit shotgun and we exchanged tales about shooting ducks – he in the Po marshes and me on what we called the 'firing line' between Lake Winnipeg and Lake Manitoba.

After we landed in Normandy, I wrote to the Major enquiring about **TONY**. He told me that my Italian friend was doing very well indeed. The peculiar coincidences with **TONY**, however, were not to end with the letters from his Major. The rest of the story of **TONY** will come later. Suffice it to say that our friendship (and I am proud to call it that) had developed when **TONY** was with **DUDLEY HESKETH**.

I had no idea that I would ever see him again, but this is a memoir.

Chapter 10

D-DAY

COMBAT ACTIONS IN CAPSULE FORM

THE LANDING OF THE RWR AT JUNO BEACH

"We were so seasick, that we had preferred to be shot on the beaches rather than go back on those landing craft."

- Rifleman Ernie Taylor, D Company, RWR

Cited hereunder are some quotes from the Regimental documents:

0400 June 6 '44 – Strong northwest winds and heavy sea. Tea and a cold snack. As the serial numbers were called the RWR boarded their respective landing craft. The tension mounted.

0515 – All LCAs now manned. Still ten miles from shore.

0655 – The supporting shells from our guys which was supposed to land on our objective at Courseulles fell short or were over the German positions. Also, we landed one hour late. Our DD tanks (floaters) failed to keep abreast of our landing craft. Not their fault. Accordingly, the regiment went in 'cold.'

0749 – Touchdown. Despite the air support, which failed to materialize, the spotty Royal Naval bombardment, the rockets falling short, and the DD tanks and armoured vehicle Royal Engineers being late, the regiment hit the beach.

On our right, C Company, with some Can Scots, landed at the junction of Mike and Love sections of Juno and headed towards the Chateau Vaux. It was unoccupied.

Major Lockie Fulton took D Company in with some Pioneers. They landed on Mike Green (western end of RWR objective). D Company headed for Graye-sur-Mer and came under only sporadic fire.

Captain Phil Gower, with extra men and two sections of 6 Field Company RCE, landed on the far left. This was the toughest objective of any on D-Day - or so we are led to believe.

Gower walked in the water without his hat, waving everyone on. We landed at a lower tide than predicted.

Lockie spoke at the 55th anniversary at Courseulles in 1999 and described the battle. He used the word 'surprised' at the lightness of the opposition.

0900 - Graye-sur-Mer: "D" for DOG company had quickly poured through a minefield at Valletta. They went through Graye and made progress to about six miles in. The main opposition was snipers, although the beach behind DOG Company was still under German artillery fire.

Freddy Hodge was commanding A Company. They moved inland following the landings of B Company (Gower) and D Company (Fulton). They came under heavy machine gun fire but continued going. C Company was under Major Jimmy Jones, and they made their way right through to Valletta, which was quite a ways in.

1400 - The intelligence officer, Lt. Dave Campbell told us that the pace was slow because there was troop congestion on the beach; hence we had no opportunity to fill the ranks of those poor devils who were killed or wounded on the actual landing.

1800 - Creully: This was a real obstacle. The small bridge was taken by Lt. Jack Mitchell and a number of Riflemen, aided by a tank from the 6th Hussars.

On the beach that evening, lifeless bodies wearing the white and black shoulder flashes of the RWR lay in the dunes. There were many Germans with the dreaded swastikas on them. They too had gone to Valhalla.

The battalion's war diary said, quite truthfully, that not one officer or man failed to display courage, energy and gallantry. Fatal casualties for the day exceeded 130. Division apparently announced that the RWR had been the first to reach its objective. Our good buddies in the Regina 'Johns' dispute this. A reconnaissance (recce) carried out afterwards found that Major **STU TUBB** of the Regina 'Johns' had, in fact, crossed the Caen-Bayeux railroad and the Route Nationale and secured the town of Norrey.

It was when, looking through the casualty list in the Regimental Aid Post (RAP) of those killed on D-Day, that the name **RFN LAWRENCE SCAIFE** came up.

A Provost Corporal directed me to **LAWRENCE (LARRY) SCAIFE'S** body. He pointed to a number of RWRs laid out at an angle of 90 degrees from the concrete wall at Juno Beach. I knelt beside **LARRY**. He did not seem to have a scratch on him - - but he certainly was dead.

LARRY weighed in at about 210 lbs. Always, he had a crooked little smile on his face. It was still there. Clearly I remember looking into the distance and asking my mothers' permission to swear (she was living in Winnipeg at that time).

In the **CHADDERTON** household when I was a kid, swearing was forbidden. It probably had something to do with the fact that my father suffered constantly from the effects of having been gassed in World War I.

LARRY SCAIFE – lying in the stillness of death – was a prime example of the cruelty of war. Knowing my mother would approve, just this once, I let loose with every blasphemous word I knew. How in God's name did we ever let this world get to the point where people like **LARRY SCAIFE**, at the age of 27, would pay - that overworked phrase - 'the supreme sacrifice.'

If the Good Lord made man in his image he certainly excelled with **LARRY**. It would have been my preference, at that point, to go on and on – swearing, cursing, shaking my fist toward the skies. Take my word for it, no finer man ever walked the earth than **LARRY SCAIFE**.

Perhaps 100 times since D-Day, I have closed my eyes and seen **LARRY SCAIFE** lying on the sand, probably very near the machine guns which he must have almost reached before a German marksman got him.

He was one of the original Rifles with a service number of H 40742. He reported to 'A' company when I was a Lance Jack (Lance Corporal) looking after the records. He was a great soldier.

His name is still in my platoon book – the one I carried with me throughout the war. What else do I remember? No one ever had to ask **LARRY SCAIFE** for a favour. It was automatic. He seemed to know what people wanted and he was willing to provide it.

One example I remember was in Debert when a vicious snow storm had blocked the doorway. **LARRY** jumped through an open window yelling "give me a rifle but take the bolt out." Still in his skivvies he went to the weather side of the door blocking our escape. Even today I can hear the thump, thump, thump as his powerful muscles attacked the build-up of ice. Next thing we knew, **LARRY** was inside. The fire had gone out. Nobody asked him but he scrounged some kindling and had a roaring fire going in no time.

My anger over **LARRY'S** death was not going to subside very easily. The next thought that went through my mind somehow eased the pain a little. His older brother George had served with the Queen's Own Cameron Highlanders of Winnipeg and had been killed at Dieppe, France on August 19 '42. Who knows if we are joined with friends when it is all over. The only comforting thought to me was that if the theology people were right, **LARRY** would be with his brother by now.

LARRY was the youngest son of Albert and Jane Scaife of Mather, Manitoba. Someone once asked how we reacted when good friends were killed. In answering I always thought of **LARRY SCAIFE** and said words to the effect that I cried like a baby. The tendency is to go through all the stages the psychiatrists talk about – one of which is denial. How could **LARRY'S** death be denied when he was lying in front of me. Larry never complained about the cards he had been dealt on this earth. He would go on joyfully, playing the game, being one of the guys. I wondered how it would be possible for me to carry on, but knew that it had to be done. For some reason I exchanged mercury helmets. His was lying beside him. I tenderly placed mine over his heart, and took his. Don't ask me the reason. His helmet did, however, serve me well for the next four months until, as I have said at the start of this memoir, I began my BORROWED TIME. Once again, dammit, dammit, someone must have said that war is no respecter of persons. If so, Larry should have been allowed to live out his 'three-score and ten'. No man more deserved to enjoy the fruits of his labours on this earth than my friend, **LAWRENCE SCAIFE**.

German prisoners guarded by Canadian troops on Juno Beach on D-Day
Courtesy of the National Archives of Canada (PA-136280)

For the rest of the story of the RWR on D-Day, personal correspondence is useful. The letter quoted hereunder is from **CAPT. PHIL GOWER**, MC, who was commanding Baker Company. He was a POW and remained in the permanent force after the war. He wrote to me from Seoul in Korea, and here is part of his letter:

Dear Cliff,

Thanks for trying to straighten out my loss of pay because I was refused major's rank. I am not bitter. I was glad to take on the job and know that John Meldrum did everything possible to get the major's position off his hands, but you-know-who was occupying that position at, I believe, 40th Div so that's that.

You have asked me to give you my thoughts on June 6th. As you know, I am a man of few words.

The first shell landed about thirty yards from our leading LCA. The smoke, noise and confusion were unbelievable. Fortunately or not, we had the biggest objective, being the pillbox at the corner of the Seulles River. From the minute the plans were opened, Cosy [Bill Aitken, platoon commander] said, "That's Cosy's bunker." I believe it is still known as that today [1953]. The bunker did not seem to be bothering us, as it was firing over our heads, although there were some lower slits and we could see muzzle flashes. The worst firing seemed to come to us from the 75mm entrenchments, anywhere from 50 to 150 yards to our right.

Frankly, I could not hear the bullets, although the mortar shells — well, you couldn't mistake them.

I landed in a muddle of platoon commanders. I never got to know the 27 guys that had been added to my company. When I looked around, however, I saw the water full of floating bodies and knew that it was the deadly machine guns that were doing most of the damage. Much was written about the fact that I took off my tin hat and waved the guys forward. The truth of the matter is I lost the darn thing, but was carrying a Sten gun which I used to wave the guys forward.

Cliff, they were fantastic. How these guys from the Depression years could fight like they did – no fears… yelling like crazy with only the objective in mind – I will never know.

The secret was to keep moving and we did this.

John Karasevich, my 2IC, seemed to be everywhere. I think he was carrying a rifle with a bayonet. That gives you some idea of his feeling for these Germans.

You will remember we were told that they were second-class troops. I said to myself, "Phil, old boy, wait 'til we hit the first-class troops!" These guys from the 127th Division may have been too old for the Russian War or whatever. They knew, though, that the dreaded Panzer battalions were behind them, so with them it was 'stand and fight and die.' A few gave up, and we tucked them in behind the stone wall along the waterway.

Much has been written about Corporal Bull Klos. Although I did not see it, I was told that he was the first down the steps. He ran into a German who shot him, and Bull – all 220 pounds of him – throttled the guy and then fell over and died – I think immediately. At least that's what I told his family in the letter I wrote.

Surprisingly, I could see the Regina Rifles across the Seulles River taking a somewhat smaller casement. There was smoke pouring out of it, and I said, "Thank God for that!" There was a marsh behind the pillbox so we consolidated that position, and then I got John and told him we had umpteen prisoners and the pillbox was ours. That's it, old buddy.

I am told I will be going to Calgary where my wife, Anne, is now staying when I finish up the little administrative job they have given me over here. I hate to say it, but I think they posted me into the Korean zone just in case we needed guys with a little experience.

Hope you are still losing at Canasta!

Phil

ROSS MUNRO, frontline reporter of The Canadian Press, in his despatch of that day, June 6 '44 wrote:

"Bloody fighting raged all along the beaches. On the right, the Winnipegs had to battle their way past five major concrete casements and 15 machine gun positions set in the dunes commanding a long sweep of beach. From dune to dune, along the German trench systems, and through the tunnels, these Manitoba troops fought every yard of the way. They broke into the casements, ferreted out the gun crews with machine guns, grenades, bayonets and knives. The Canadians ran into cross-fire. They were shelled and mortared even in the German positions, but they kept slugging away at the enemy. After a struggle that was ... bitter and savage ... the Winnipeg's broke through into the open country behind the beach."

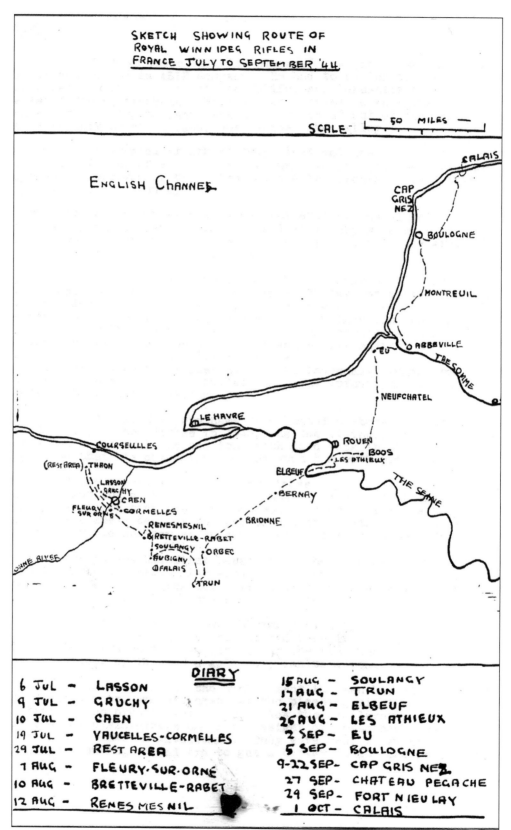

SKETCH SHOWING ROUTE OF
ROYAL WINNIPEG RIFLES IN
FRANCE JULY TO SEPTEMBER '44

SCALE — 50 MILES —

ENGLISH CHANNEL

CALAIS
CAP GRIS NEZ
BOULOGNE
MONTREUIL
ABBEVILLE
THE SOMME
EU
NEUFCHATEL
LE HAVRE
ROUEN
BOOS
LES ATHIEUX
COURSEULLES
ELBEUF
THE SEINE
(REST AREA) THAON
LASSON
GRUCHY
CAEN
FLEURY SUR ORNE
CORMELLES
BERNAY
BRIONNE
RENESMESNIL
BRETTEVILLE-RABET
SOULANGY
ORBEC
AUBIGNY
FALAIS
ORNE RIVER
TRUN

DIARY

6 JUL –	LASSON	15 AUG –	SOULANGY
9 JUL –	GRUCHY	17 AUG –	TRUN
10 JUL –	CAEN	21 AUG –	ELBEUF
19 JUL –	VAUCELLES-CORMELLES	25 AUG –	LES ATHIEUX
29 JUL –	REST AREA	2 SEP –	EU
7 AUG –	FLEURY-SUR-ORNE	5 SEP –	BOULOGNE
10 AUG –	BRETTEVILLE-RABET	9-22 SEP –	CAP GRIS NEZ
12 AUG –	RENES MESNIL	27 SEP –	CHATEAU PEGACHE
		29 SEP –	FORT NIEULAY
		1 OCT –	CALAIS

Extracted from Diary of
Capt. H.C. Chadderton, Royal Winnipeg Rifles

Page 36

Chapter 11

THE RWR GOES INLAND

Shame us with broken oaths we swore the dead
But steadfast in humility we rise
Hoping no glory, having merited none

Siegfried Sassoon

THE CROSSROADS

Any foot slogger who says he can tell you exactly where he was during D plus 2 would be a candidate for the old saying from the radio program *Fibber McGee and Molly*. Those with memories of the thirties will recall Molly, replying to Fibber McGee when he told one of his long nose-stretchers: "You're a better man than me, McGee."

The crossroads referred to here was really difficult to pinpoint on our map. It was at the juncture of two of the so-called 'sunken roads' which crisscrossed the area about seven or eight miles inland from the beachhead.

Our carrier platoon was dug in, with orders to defend this particular crossroads. We had about six of our carriers placed in strategic but haphazard positions, ready to repel any Germans who came near. The CO wanted to keep that crossroads in Canadian hands. I would like to say that we were a very orderly bunch, but that just ain't the truth!

There were ten to twenty stragglers from other regiments around us.

As well, about ten German prisoners were in our hands. They had been sent back from the forward areas. **JOE SAKOLINSKI** from Brandon, Manitoba arrived with the nasty-looking Germans at rifle point. It is interesting to conjecture as to how one little private soldier could herd ten of the toughest-looking Nazis through country where they could easily have escaped. They were dissuaded from doing so by the look in **SAKOLINSKI'S** eyes, also by the fact that every now and again (quite by accident, one might suppose) he fired a round or two at the Germans' jackboots. It could not be said that they were scared. My guess is, however, that most of them could stand a change of underwear.

SAKOLINSKI was reluctant to take the Germans back any further. The fact that he was Jewish had something to do with it. He asked whether we could leave them under his guard. He would position himself behind their slit trenches (called fox holes in the American Army). God help any who tried to get away. As we were short-handed; my answer was YES. **SAKO** was happy to keep them under his wing.

One of the incidents at this crossroads taught me a lesson. An ambulance jeep came roaring down the road from our forward area. It drew a dangerous dust storm, and Jerry decided to have some fun trying to pick us off. I waved the jeep into a ditch. It was carrying **MAJ STU TUBB** of the Regina Rifles. We had often trained with the Reginas and I knew **STU** from those Brigade schemes in England. They involved the Regina 'Johns,' the Can Scots, and our Battalion.

STU had lost a leg and was being sent back for medical attention. A German mortar had landed beside the carrier and **STU** took the blast. Although he was in bad condition, he motioned me over and asked if I was with the carrier platoon. I said yes. He advised never to get under a carrier as there was no protection from German shelling. I thanked **STU** and saw him on his way. His warning stayed with us. Not under any circumstances did anyone crawl under a carrier if shells were falling. We learned first to dig a very deep slit trench and run the carrier over top. This protected us from the blast.

Another incident at the crossroads is worth telling. It concerns a runner by the name of **JOHNNY DOUCETTE** from Jacquet River, New Brunswick. He had earned his pre-war living as a woodsman. There were certain areas in our battlefield which he said were very dangerous. How did he know? He pointed to his nose - he could smell them. At the next junction of sunken roads, **JOHN** gave the 'no go there' signal. It got a wide berth. Sure enough, at that particular spot, the Germans laid down a mortar and artillery shoot. Our section could have been wiped out.

One more incident - some of our vehicles had gone ahead. The lead carrier driver came back and said that we should not follow any previous tracks. This caused some wonder. If a vehicle had gone ahead of us, the tracks were presumably safe. **JOE MOZUK** then told about a nasty trick of the Germans. They had mines which could be set to go off only after face plates had been depressed five or six times. Therefore, a number of vehicles could go over the mines and suffer no harm. Heaven help the next vehicle that came along. As the ratchet in the primed mine reached its bottom level, it would explode. Another Canadian vehicle and its crew would pay the price.

One of the most comical sights occurred on our route inland from the coast. Coming over the brow of the hill was the CSM's carrier from A Company. In the leading vehicle, standing up and challenging every German in sight was **CSM CARL BROWN** of A Coy (Company), shouting "Get out of our goddamn way!" Driving the carrier, I believe, was **GRANT SUCHE** – small, tough, maybe reminiscent of a bulldog.

Hanging over the vehicle's front was a sign. It said – THROUGH, AROUND OR STRAIGHT UP THE GODDAMN MIDDLE. What would any English speaking German SS think if the A Company carrier attacked their position in Putot?

My first encounter using the carrier was a lesson in how NOT to fight a war. My orders were to touch base with **LT SEWELL** of the Inns of Court Regiment. **JOE MOZUK**, my driver, was going all out up a hill. We were given a map reference indicating where we would meet with the Inns of Court Regiment which was on high ground looking south. We passed them. Their vehicles were well concealed. We then did a 180°. Surprise! My carrier, belting back along a country road, came head to head with **LT SEWELL** standing nonchalantly holding a cigarette in a long silver holder. He laughed and asked, "What kept you, old boy?" As we sat chatting, we saw the Germans attacking the bridge across the Caen-Bayeux railway tracks.

We were about one-half mile north of Putot-en-Bessin – a small village consisting of farms, one or two administration buildings, and a church. There was a small bridge (Brouay) at the western end. **MAJ FRED HODGE** of A Company had been ordered to attack the Germans holding this bridge position.

LT SEWELL, still leaning on his scout car, suddenly perked up. He was looking through his field glasses and noted swarms of Germans crossing the railroad tracks from the south and coming between our position and the defensive position which **LT COL JOHN MELDRAM** had established in Putot.

Excitement set in. **LT SEWELL**, an experienced officer who had fought in the desert, said to *stay put*. "Tell your CO and get your vehicles under cover."

The Germans had encircled the RWR position. Our troops put up a short fight – particularly those in the orchard, from which they had no field of fire.

Both Baker and Charlie Companies occupied this ground. The company commander, **MAJ JIMMY JONES**, had established his headquarters at the rear of the town and was able to use his carrier for a 'getaway.'

This left **CAPT BILL SAUL** in charge. A man of unusual bravery and action, **BILL** organized a fighting patrol and headed back towards the beaches with about twenty of his men. (His son, **JOHN RALSTON SAUL**, is the husband of our current Governor General, **ADRIENNE CLARKSON**.)

We watched the German grey-green horde turn, encircle and trap our B and C Companies which had occupied a fenced-in farm and an orchard. Fortunately, our tactical headquarters was at the eastern end of Putot. The German encircling movement was stopped by Dog Company, under the command of **MAJ LOCKIE FULTON**. They then turned south toward their own lines.

In the meantime, **LT SEWELL**, in a cool, collected voice which only a cultured Englishman develops, told his CO of the situation. He stayed on the radio network to keep the Germans under observation. His reports went to the Green Howards of the British 40th Division. In the meantime, our CO, **LT COL MELDRAM**, ordered us to take up a watching detail at a crossroads where the North Shore Regiment was expected to come through.

Rescue Behind Enemy Lines

RFN DAVE SABISTON of Pine Falls, Manitoba, a despatch rider with my platoon, was given the task of taking a motorcycle behind the German position at Putot to report back on their dispositions. A captured German prisoner who was interrogated by us had **SABISTON'S** dog tags with him. He said he thought **SABISTON** was wounded, and he gave the approximate location. Without asking, **Sewell** took two of his scout cars and beetled straight south, right through the German armoured positions. As he had predicted, the Germans did not fire at him. He had the map reference, found **Dave**, and brought him back. We took him to our own Regimental Aid Post for attention. Unfortunately **Dave Sabiston** died on June 12 '44,. He is buried at the Canadian Military Cemetery at Bretteville. *Sabiston Lake* (64 N/16), west of Nueltin Lake, was named after him in 1972.

As an adjunct to the Inns of Court, I am indebted to **Lt. Sewell** for giving me sound advice on the basic tactics of an armoured scout mission. Naturally, we were anxious to engage the enemy. We thought that was our job. **Sewell** sketched out for me in his notepad how an armoured vehicle with fast wheels or tracks could be most effective. We could plunge ahead with impunity. The Germans would not touch us because they thought that there would be a larger formation coming from behind. Once we found out what we wanted, we could get on the radio set, tell our own tactical headquarters the situation, then circle back on another route.

Meanwhile at A Coy there was excitement. **Corp H.V. Naylor's** anti-tank platoon had bagged a German MK III tank. Their joy was, however, short-lived because the bridge was overrun and the Germans were taking prisoners down a road in a westerly direction to a large château.

An observation is in order here. The officers of the Inns of Court Regiment were all lawyers. The NCOs were, I was later told, the pick of the crop who had come back from the desert war. They were tough. They knew their weapons and they were experts at the manoeuvring of their scout cars. In the little time we were together, I had the opportunity to note how they regarded the rough, tough Canadians. There was an immediate rapport. By the way, **Lt Sewell** was a ballet dancer as well as a barrister.

Maj Fred Hodge

The first three RWRs were captured on the morning of June 8 '44 at the Brouay Bridge at the Western end of Putot. They included **Maj Fred Hodge**, who is believed to be among the first Canadian officers captured. They were marched to the headquarters of a German recce unit. The importance of the interrogation of these three prisoners was crucial for the Germans.

The German High Command was still not sure where the final landing would take place. Evidence at a later Court of Inquiry, given by a Polish German SS conscript (good guy), and by the two French girls who were witnesses, was that **FRED HODGE** gave the traditional order in accordance with the Geneva Convention. He turned to the other two soldiers and said, "Rank, name and serial number." The German SS sergeant shot him in the face, decapitating him. In part it was because, as a Canadian officer, he had no serial number to give[1]. The other two were summarily dispatched by the German-held Schmeissers.

German Schmeisser

Hodge Bay (64 P/15) in Coutts Lake, Manitoba, was named after *MAJ FRED HODGE* in 1989.

LOCKIE FULTON and Dog Company were far enough east so that the German encircling movement was forced to turn back south. They were repelled when **LT JACK BENHAM'S** platoon called down our own mortars, reinforced by some of the larger 4.2 mortars and Vickers machine guns of the Cameron Highlanders of Ottawa. **BENHAM'S** troops, using rifles, grenades, Bren guns and Sten guns, added enough firepower to convince the Germans that there was no point in going further east. They retreated back across the railway embankment to their own start line area.

Later that day, 58 Winnipeg Rifles and others were herded into a field south of the Château d'Audrieu. The notorious German SS **GEN WILHELM MOHNKE** saw the Canadians as he was driving by. He lined up two mobile Jerry vehicles armed with fixed Spandau MGs. Two officers (**LT BILL FERGUSON**, RWR and **TOM WINDSOR**, Sherbrooke Fusiliers) told the captured men to be quiet as their lives might be saved. The two courageous officers were cut down as they started towards **MOHNKE**. The rest of the RWRs and several soldiers from other units had been disarmed

---

[1] Canadian Army Officers did not use service numbers.

and personal effects taken from them. They were practically annihilated by murderous MG fire as they scattered. Most were killed (five escaped).

BILL FERGUSON is commemorated by the naming of *Ferguson Island* (63 N/11) in Morin Lake, Manitoba.

It was heart-sickening to see Canadian boys, with whom I had soldiered for many months, cut down – with no chance to defend themselves.

The bodies of the RWRs and other Canadians murdered in the Château d'Audrieu area were discovered by *CAPT LLOYD SNEATH*. He had been a Non-Commissioned Officer with the RWRs and had transferred to a British Regiment. The posting to the Hallamshire Battalion of the Lancaster and York Regiment was under the CanLoan scheme which provided Canadian officers to fill vacancies in the British Army.

The monument in Normandy is built into a wall near the Château d'Audrieu. Their names are listed as follows:

CANADA

TO THE MEMORY OF THOSE MEMBERS OF THE ROYAL WINNIPEG RIFLES AND SUPPORTING ARMS WHO WERE MURDERED, WHILE PRISONERS OF WAR AT LE CHATEAU D'AUDRIEU NEAR LE MESNIL-PATRY, AND AT LE HAUT DU BOSQ. ON 8, 9 AND 11 JUNE 1944.

ROYAL WINNIPEG RIFLES

H 41531	RFN	ADAMS, W.C.	H 17557	CPL	KYLE, J.F.
H 1797	RFN	BASKERVILLE, E.C.	H 103987	RFN	LABRECQUE, H.A.
H 10721	RFN	BIRSTON, H.J.H.	H 1170	RFN	LAWRENCE, K.S.
H 1463	RFN	BISHOFF, E.	H 41815	RFN	LEFORT, E.J.
H 104452	RFN	BOOTH, W.J.	H 41029	RFN	LEWIS, G.J.
H 103409	RFN	BRADLEY, E.W.	A 107694	RFN	LYCHOWICH, J.L.
H 40785	CPL	BROWN, G.A.	H 40564	RFN	MACLEOD, A.M.
H 41247	RFN	CHARTRAND, L.	H 41558	RFN	MARYCH, F.
H 41294	RFN	CHARTRAND, L.	H 102744	RFN	MCINTOSH, J.D.
K 83541	RFN	CRESSWELL, S.J.	H 95615	L/CPL	MEAKIN, F.V.
H 41713	L/CPL	CULLETON, S.	H 40752	CPL	MEAKIN, G.E.
H 41582	RFN	DANIELS, W.	L 104718	RFN	MORRISON, W.K.
H 41980	RFN	FAGNAN, A.A.	H 1777	RFN	MUTCH, R.
	LT	FERGUSON, W.S.	H 42014	RFN	OSTIR, F.

B 131123	RFN	FINDLAY, R.M.	L 105551	RFN	OWENS, A.R.
H 40587	CPL	FIRMAN, R.J.	H 100792	RFN	PARISIAN, P.
H 14610	RFN	FREEMAN, L.	H 20430	RFN	PETERSON, A.M.
H 41280	L/CPL	FULLER, A.R.	H 9437	L/CPL	POHO, W.
H 16928	RFN	GOLD, D.S.	H 40798	SGT	REID, J.A.
H 40925	RFN	GRAHAM, J.W.	H 8918	RFN	RODGERS, H.
H 42018	RFN	GUIBOCHE, L.R.	L 100881	RFN	RYCKMAN, F.
L 105515	RFN	HARPER, R.J.	H 40931	CPL	SCOTT, R.
B 138308	RFN	HARRISON, F.D.	H 8899	RFN	SIGURDSON, K.
H 40561	L/CPL	HILL, J.W.	H 21123	RFN	SLYWCHUK, S.
	MAJ	HODGE, F.E.	H 42084	RFN	SMITH, E.
B 79614	RFN	HOLNESS, F.W.G.	B 32922	RFN	SMITH, F.
B 87928	RFN	HORTON, C.A.	B 138331	RFN	SMITH, R.G.
B 117027	RFN	JONES, H.C.	H 40697	RFN	THOMAS, W.D.
H 41150	L/CPL	KINES, C.D.	L 103385	RFN	THOMPSON, J.A.

6TH FIELD COMPANY R.C.E.

B 25464	SPR	BENNER, G.A.	B 142277	SPR	IONEL, J.

3RD ANTI-TANK REGIMENT R.C.A.

	LT	BARKER, R.D.	E 21962	L/SGT	BERESFORD, W.
H 45602	BDR	GRANT, T.J.D.	B 112474	GNR	HARKNESS, A.J.J.

CAMERON HIGHLANDERS OF OTTAWA (M.G.)

C 21411	PTE	ANGEL, H.S.	G 32757	PTE	BURNETT, D.J.

What about retaliation by our men? During four months of combat, I never saw a Canadian shoot a German who had surrendered. Neither did I see a regular German soldier of the Wehrmacht shoot a Canadian in cold blood. The murders were the work of the notorious 12th SS Hitler Jugend (Hitler Youth) who refused to take an oath to the German Army. They swore allegiance only to Adolf Hitler.

There was great interest regarding Hitler's generals who were responsible for the murders. SS **GEN WILHELM MOHNKE** was never apprehended. He was CO of the 26th Panzer Grenadier Regiment. We have pictures of him in 1985 living out a life of retirement in Stemwarde, East Germany.

In December '45, **GEN KURT MEYER** of the 12th SS was tried, found guilty and sentenced to death. The Canadian General in command, the ferocious-looking **CHRIS VOKES**, proudly known as the most profane man in the Canadian Army, commuted the sentence to life in prison.

A few years later, after his early release from German prison, **KURT MEYER** was in a Canadian Officer's mess in Germany. He had bellied up to the bar and was seen sketching out on a napkin how the Germans were superior at planning military manoeuvres. Hundreds of thousands of well-trained German troops could testify as to how the German defence plans failed. **KURT MEYER** (who died on December 23 '61) must have been mistaken. History records that the Canadians must have been good enough to defeat the Germans!

Kurt Meyer flanked by his officer - - Kurt Meyer Trial

Because of the notoriety of the **KURT MEYER** trial and its aftermath, many Canadians – even some historians among them – are of the opinion that the murders of the RWR were the work of **KURT MEYER**. This is not true. His trial concerned the deaths of members of the North Nova Scotia Highlanders and the Sherbrooke Fusiliers. The impression that Meyer was involved with the murder of RWRs probably arose from the fact that he was tried at the military barracks in Aurich, Germany, which was occupied at the time by the RWR. Pictures of the trial showed two RWR officers (**BILL STUTT** and **ART RUSSELL**) as his guards. In particular, **ART RUSSELL** is identified by the 'Royal Winnipeg Rifles' shoulder flash.

A postscript by War Correspondent Ross Munro . . .

This at or near Château d'Audrieu . . . A shameful episode in war. The number of Royal Winnipeg Rifles who were murdered on <u>D plus 2</u> during the first battle at Brouay Bridge guarding the Caen-Bayeux railroad and, as a second horror, the Royal Winnipeg Rifles who were murdered the next day as they were supposedly being marched to the German compound for interrogation and incarceration as prisoners of war, tells much about the Hitler Youth – the worst of the German SS.

Putot was a strategically important objective. **BRIGADIER HARRY FOSTER**, commanding the 7th Brigade, realized it had to be recaptured quickly. He gave the job to the Can Scots. If one goes through the area today, there are plaques: one to mark the defence put up by the RWRs; the other to commemorate the re-taking of Putot by the Can Scots.

This narrative is not complete without mention of the bravery of a number of RWRs. **CAPT BASIL BROWN** was shot in his slit trench as he tried to organize a defence. **LT LEW McQUEEN** decided on his own to organize a fighting patrol toward the German lines. He was the first man out of the railway cutting. I saw his body lying just past the railway tracks. It was partly covered by sod, branches and leaves.

BASIL BROWN is commemorated by the naming of *Basil Brown Lake* (64 N/1) west of Minuhik Lake. **LEW McQUEEN** is commemorated by the naming of *McQueen Lake* (54 K/12) located southeast of Churchill.

LT JACK BENHAM, who with his men fought savagely, stood off the attacking Germans, thus preventing capture of Dog Company and Battalion Headquarters. **JACK** was killed on June 8 '44 at the age of 31. He is buried in the Bretteville-sur-Laize Canadian War Cemetery. He is memorialized by the naming of *Benham Lake* (64 N/12) located in the northwest corner of Manitoba near the border with Nunavut.

In a firefight like this, heroes were plentiful – both officers and other ranks. It was not possible to identify most of the dead bodies of RWRs in and around Putot.

Chapter 12

A BATMAN TAKES COMMAND

Truth sits upon the lips of dying men.

Mathew Arnold

No description of the RWR soldier would be complete without mention of **RFN ARTHUR DESJARLAIS**.

Reference is made elsewhere in this story of the two companies of the Winnipegs which were surrounded and taken prisoner on June 8 '44. Most of them were shot while POWs.

LT LEW MCQUEEN ... a former brilliant NCO promoted to Lieutenant was quick to act, realizing his platoon and company were pinned down. **MCQUEEN** resorted to a dangerous but necessary tactic – get your men under cover and bring down your own artillery and mortar fire on your position, hoping to drive Jerry out. He turned to **ARTHUR DESJARLAIS**, his batman (runner) and explained the plan. Desjarlais was quick to go along. He was dismayed, however, when **LT MCQUEEN** was hit by a sniper as he attempted to crawl out of the railway embankment which formed the Southern border of the orchard.

When **MCQUEEN** succumbed to the German fire – a bullet in the gut - **DESJARLAIS** took over. He was a well-liked Métis who had been with the Regiment almost from the beginning. He messaged the Mortar Platoon Commander, **CAPT ANDY BIEBER** (a former CFL All-Star) to increase the fire.

Realizing that the situation was hopeless, **DESJARLAIS**, in a move to save lives, told the remainder of the platoon to surrender - this from a courageous company runner.

The survivors of the two platoons (B and C) were marched South, until halted by German NCOs and herded into a field. **GEN WILHELM MOHNKE**, from his staff car, issued an order to shoot the nearly 60 Winnipeg Rifles and others, even though they had been disarmed and taken as POW's under the rules of the Geneva Convention.

DESJARLAIS stood up, shook his fists at the Germans with their Spandaus and told the captured Canadians to scatter.

ART DESJARLAIS was one of five Canadians who made it to a nearby wheat field. The next day he was taken prisoner and sent to a POW camp.

Several years later he gave telling information at the trial of the two German Officers (MAJ GERHARD BREMER and SS CAPT GORD VON REIGZENSTEIN) both of whom were hung for their crimes.

A copy of DESJARLAIS' evidence is in the papers at the Canadian Archives. He returned to Winnipeg to live a quiet life. If prompted, he would tell the story of his escape and his evidence before the War Crimes Trials. He gave the impression, however, that he would just as soon forget the entire episode.

Think of it! DESJARLAIS was typical of the calibre of runners who were on the company records as batmen. Superior young officers like LEW MCQUEEN would choose them, not because it would be a question of 'who polishes whose shoes.' Rather, MCQUEEN selected DESJARLAIS because of his native cunning, his courage and, quite possibly, the knowledge that if anything happened to him, DESJARLAIS would take over - which he did.

Chapter 13

WALTER RATINSKY

The bells of hell go ting-a-ling-a-ling,
For you but not for me.
And the little devils how thy sing-a-ling-a-ling,
For you but not for me.
O death, where is they sting-a-ling-a-ling,
O grave, they victory?
The bells of hell go ting-a-ling-a-ling,
For you but not for me.

WWI Trench Song

Early in July '40, a truckload of recruits came into the RWR headquarters located in the old Robinson department store building near Portage and Main in downtown Winnipeg. The six-storey structure had been in disuse since the business failed during the mid-thirties Depression.

It was a busy day in the battalion headquarters when in came this good-looking, well-built fellow. He reacted rather strongly when I asked his name. He said it was ROHATYNSKI. Leafing through some files – and sensing some resistance over the spelling of his name – he suggested it had been a problem all of his life. He was a bright guy. He had come to the Winnipeg recruiting office on a draft from the small town of Morden, 60-odd miles west of Winnipeg. It is easily discernible as to his enlistment date by his regimental number, which was H 41254.

When he was told that he could certainly enlist under the family name of ROHATYNSKI, the suggestion was also made that he could change it. The spelling of names was a problem, particularly for a battalion from Western Canada where those enlisting were made up of a number of different racial backgrounds such as Ukrainian, German, Métis (more about this group later) and a goodly number of Icelanders from the settlement at Gimli, Manitoba, 75 miles north of Winnipeg.

ROHATYNSKI was in a bit of turmoil, so I invited him out for a beer. The problem was that he really wanted to change his name, but he was not about to take our word for it. Turning to a recruiting pamphlet, he was shown that the authority for a change in name certainly existed. I also let him in on a little secret - many of those wanting to enlist were adamant that they be allowed to use a false name, possibly to confuse family members or escape from a questionable background. After the fourth or fifth ale, I suggested we reduce the name to RATINSKY – easy to say, easy to spell. WALTER brightened up immediately.

Several months later, I was transferred to a company where WALTER was fast becoming known as a good soldier. As we towelled off after a cold shower in Camp Shilo, he turned to me and said "Some friend you turned out to be, I traded a perfectly good name for RATINSKY. You might have told me!" With the Army's propensity for nicknames, he was asking for trouble – and had become known, in a friendly way, as 'Walter the Rat.'

RFN WALTER RATINSKY was what you might call the 'ordinary' rifleman – if there was such a thing. He was killed on July 4 '44 at the battle of Carpiquet Airport. The battle of Carpiquet was a huge blunder. The staff used one battalion plus supporting arms. It would have taken a whole division to dislodge the 12th SS from the high ground behind the airport hangars. Our carriers were lined up in a ditch at the north end of the airfield when a smiling face looked up, waved and said: "Hey, it's Wally the Rat." I hardly recognized him. He had always looked good, but by now he might be described as 'every inch a soldier.'

Following is an account from CAPT BRIAN ROBERTSON, at the time commanding the platoon in which RATINSKY was a standout soldier in a letter to a bereaved Mother:

Dear Mrs. Ratinsky: I would like to take this opportunity of giving what information I can on Walter's death and sending the sympathies of myself and the platoon in your loss. He was killed instantly by a mortar bomb during an enemy barrage. I was in the next trench and as soon as the barrage stopped I went over to him and I know that his death must have been instant and that he could have suffered no pain. We buried him the same day and the Padre came down and held a service which many of the lads in the platoon attended. His grave was carefully marked and as soon as the battle moves forward from that area he will be moved to a military cemetery.

The loss to me was particularly great as he was part of my headquarters and as a result I knew him very well and know what a grand fellow he was. His work in the platoon was excellent and having been in the platoon for so long he was very well known and liked by everyone. Knowing what a loss his death has been to us, we know how much harder it must be for you and I hope that you will have some consolation in the fact that he has left us for a better world after doing his part in this great fight. (13 July 1944)

WALTER RATINSKY was killed in the middle of the airfield. It was a sad occasion when I saw the stretcher-bearers bringing back his body. He is buried in Beny-sur-Mer Canadian War Cemetery. The geographical location chosen by the Manitoba Historical Sites Board is *Ratinsky Lake* (64 N/4), located north of Lac Brochet.

WALTER'S story is remarkable for many reasons, not the least of which is the brilliant description of being in the middle of a literal maelstrom of Nebelwerfer shells (the Canadians called them Moaning Minnies – either a six- or twelve-barrel machine of death, the name came from the roar they made as they went overhead). At that time, the RWR had been in action about four weeks – long enough to recognize the various noises of battle. Moaning Minnies were one thing. A German .88, known as the best field gun for land troops in World War II, made a zipping sound, assuming the shell missed. The German Spandaus were tripod-mounted fast-firing machine guns. The Schmeissers were the equivalent of (but much better than) our handheld Sten guns.

The best description of the Carpiquet battle was written by reporter **H.M. HALTON**. Halton's full description is reprinted herein:

There are no adequate adjectives for such a barrage. Tens of thousands of 25-pounder shells came over with the high wailing whistle of lost demons. The bigger shells came over with 10,000 maddened, warbling rushings. The huge naval shells came over like hell's express trains hurtling derailed through space with terrifying reverberations. Literally the earth shook and quivered and the noise was atrocious. For two hours it never ceased. The roaring of guns was bad enough, but worse was the explosion of the scores of thousands of shells just below us in an area only a mile wide and less than two miles deep. Within a few seconds and for the next hour we could see nothing but a dense fog of smoke and cordite fumes and flames. Vomit after vomit of flame and 10,000 flashes came from the enemy positions. Really, I was appalled and thought "Men just can't do this to each other, not even to Germans. It's monstrous." And even in that frantic excitement and evil exhilaration I kept thinking, "My God, if only we could harness this demonic energy to peace."

I shook my head aghast but excited. Here was battle in all of its frightful reality – those were men down there! – so real that it seemed unreal. Men of flesh and blood attacking through that enemy shellfire and machine-gun fire, supported by a wall of fire and through a wall of fire. I forgot the microphone in hand until MacDonald shouted: "Why aren't you talking?"

I saw a terrible splendour. It was said in the last war and it is said in this that Canadians are superb assault troops. I knew this now for myself because I saw the superb in being before my eyes, a few hundred yards away, as the Canadians came towards us with their mothering tanks, in the maelstrom, through flame and steel. Nothing stopped them – NOTHING. No man stopped unless killed or wounded. I would fix my eyes on 15 or 20 men moving with a tank. Two or three mortar shells would burst among them and for a few seconds smoke would hide them from view. We would see the smoke and flame and then two seconds later hear the awful slow splitting carrumphs. But when the smoke lifted there were the easterners* advancing like automatons. Not running; walking steady as robots. Perhaps they were shouting or swearing but I couldn't hear that. I could hear only the maelstrom.

The woods from which the second wave of Canadians was coming was aflame. Some of our Bren carriers were hit and burst into flame; occasionally a tank was hit and stopped. But still the attackers bore down on Carpiquet – like fate – firing as they came. "My God, how do they do it?" I asked. "Because in war there's nothing for good men to do but go on" said Major Crofton. "You go on in spite of hell. War is like that. It's a hard and bloody thing."

Author's note: As a participant in this battle, it is possible to say that the description given by **MATTHEW HALTON** is the best word picture of what it was like to be in the middle of a hail of flat-trajectory shells and machine gun bullets. As **GEORGE HAYWARD**, a stretcher-bearer, described it ... "a tree? Not even a bloody twig." Halton tells how the battle failed but tells of the courage of the Canadians.

MAJ LOCKIE FULTON, the bravest leader we had, led the advance across the bullet-swept airfield. After the second charge, he told the CO there was no alternative but to retire his company while there were a few left. This major, standing ramrod straight (noticeably because he was more than six feet tall), walked fearlessly among the troops who were trying to take cover in shallow holes dug by shells. **FULTON** told the men to run back to the start point at Marcelet. That day, he saved many lives. **HALTON'S** despatch is a classic gem of war reporting.

---

* Canadian

Chapter 14

HIT HIM FOR SIX (A CRICKET TERM)
GEN. MONTGOMERY'S FAVOURITE SAYING

*Future years will never know the seething hell and the
black infernal background, the countless minor scenes
and interiors of the secession war; and it is best they should not.
The real war will never get in the books.*

Walt Whitman

RFN EDWARD 'ZAD' ZADWORNY was an original with the Rifles … that is to say, he had a regimental number which indicated he was in the first group to enlist. He had been in several infantry companies in the unit. Just before embarking for Normandy he walked up to our carrier, eyeing my .38 pistol.

In his mind it was 'sheer stupidity' to give an officer a revolver instead of a rifle or portable machine gun. He proceeded to chastise the military brass for asking an officer to carry only a sidearm, noting that it would be a dead giveaway for a German sniper who wanted to knock off the 'man in charge.'

Eventually ZADWORNY came out with the story. He said he had little faith in the Sten gun but would carry one on the assault. He would not, however, be able to accomplish his personal objective. For this he would need a pistol.

By this time the rest of the carrier crew gathered around. ZAD informed the group that the Germans had taken six years out of his life … he would be satisfied only if he could look at least one German square in the eye and march him back to the landing craft, saying it would be 'too easy' to shoot him. Happily holstering my .38, he went back to his company.

Curiosity was running high on the evening of D-Day. It didn't take long to find ZADWORNY'S long, chunky frame. He was wounded, not seriously. A few careful enquiries elicited the information that he had killed at least six

Germans. One had a hole from a .38 pistol round in his forehead. It had been fired at close quarters.

ED ZADWORNY was the kind of Canadian soldier members of the Wehrmacht hoped they would <u>not</u> encounter in defending Normandy.

He was killed on the open landing strip while taking part in the attack at Carpiquet Airport on 5 July '44. *Zadworny Lake* (64 I/16), northwest of North Knife Lake in Manitoba was named after him.

Incidentally, **ZAD** had to wait some 60 years for any recognition he had earned as a 'gunman' in the D-Day landing. Macleans, in it's 60th Anniversary of D-Day issue, used a photograph of his headstone in Beny-sur-Mer Cemetery. It seemed necessary to devote a chapter to describe just how tough the **ZADWORNYS** in our Regiment were. To use an expression from the days when I was a police reporter in Winnipeg, it would not be wise to pick a fight with **ZADWORNY** in a dark alley. **ZAD** got his six!

Chapter 15

ARTICLE FROM J.A.M. COOK
(and a description of the carrier)

July 14, 1944. An interesting episode – War correspondent J.A.M. Cook of the *Regina Leader-Post* asked me to take him to the RWR headquarters. An excerpt from his story appears hereunder:

Caen Is Quiet For A Change
With the Canadians in Normandy, July 12. (Special Cable)

--Furious fighting had swung south of Odon Wednesday where some of our Canadians were teamed with the British and there was hot shell fire over and around the Carpiquet airport.

But here in Caen it was at last quieter and aside from the occasional Nazi recce plane and a few airbursts of shells, the morning was a change, and the boys from one of our Scot regiments and ack ack battery from Regina were setting up their headquarters around the corner of the suburban area.

CLIFF CHADDERTON used to work for the Canadian Press in Winnipeg, but he is now a carrier officer for a Canadian infantry unit, and when we saw him he was with his outfit at the edge of Caen.

He jumped on his motorbike and said he would guide us to unit headquarters and we followed him through blasted streets into the downtown district, where a wide strip had been gouged out of the landscape in the course of battle, and presently we came to a big square and went into a stone building with a broken door, went up to the counter and met a colonel we had known back in Surrey more than a year ago.

The Carrier Tracked Vehicle

The Universal Carrier used by units from Britain and other countries of the British Commonwealth is still a matter of debate. Experience in Normandy proved that the swift tracked vehicle could serve a number of purposes. The carrier crews were the eyes and ears when radio communications were down. The carrier is valuable for reconnaissance (recce). Also the vehicle could be modified for special purpose, e.g., to bring flamethrowers into action, when needed.

Chapter 16

CARPIQUET AIRPORT

I have a rendezvous with Death
At some disputed barricade…

- Alan Seeger, American poet

The action leading up to the capture of Caen was 'hairy,' to say the least. An officer with whom I had gone through the officer cadet training unit was my contact. His name was **HERB EVOY**. He told me that the Reginas had captured the Abbaye d'Ardenne. Many years afterwards I ran into **HERB**. I believe he was a postmaster in a small Saskatchewan town. The Post Mortems were sad as we talked about our 'classmates' who would never see home again.

Concerning Carpiquet, the operation at the airport hangars and landing strip was in the hands of **MAJ LOCKIE FULTON**, the commanding officer of our Dog Company. The situation was hopeless. The German 88s commanded a field of fire across the entire tarmac. **LOCKIE** was seen standing in the middle of the airport runway, directing traffic. He told our troops to take the wounded if possible and retire to the starting point at Marcelet.

At the height of the battle, **MAJ DES CROFTON** of the Canadian Scottish Regiment took his life in his hands by running and asking **FULTON** if he needed any help. This was the conversation reported:

Crofton to Fulton: "There's nothing the Scots can do to get you out of here. From what I see, your attackers are bearing down on Carpiquet – like fate – firing as they come. My God, how do they do it?"

Fulton to Crofton: "We've got to get out of here. How do they do it? Because in war there's nothing for good men to do but go on. You go on in spite of hell. War is like that. It's a hard and bloody thing."

The RWR Carrier Platoon played a special role. Orders were to proceed from Marcelet back to the rear area; then to find and marry up with the North Shores. On the road, in a stretcher atop the framework of a modified jeep, was **LT. BARRY LEIPSIC**, whom I had known at the University of Manitoba. He had been badly wounded in the face while fighting with the Fort Garry Horse at the far side of Carpiquet Airport. The medics thought that **BARRY** would live - which he did - against seemingly impossible odds from the look of his wounds.

It took our carriers four hours to reach the North Shore Regiment. The route between Marcelet and the Southern part of Carpiquet village was marked by 'Maple Leaf Route' signs put out by traffic control staff. They usually indicated a safe passage. Not so this time. The area was under direct observation of Jerrie's formidable 88s, who were positioned on the high ground near the hangars of the airport. An officer jumped out of a slit trench in a ditch and said it would be foolish to go further as the North Shore attack was stalled. The officer was **MAJ CHET MACRAE** of the North Shore Regiment from New Brunswick. His actions probably saved us. In doing so, he had brazenly exposed himself to German snipers. He stood his ground long enough to tell us that Carpiquet was impenetrable.

The Germans had laid down fixed fields of fire. All of the access areas into the town were well-zoned for their 81mm mortars. The North Shores had named the town of Carpiquet 'the graveyard of the regiment.' It was with just cause. **MAJ MACRAE**, who later became a Member of Parliament in Ottawa, saved a lot of lives that day – including soldiers of his own regiment – and my own carrier force.

Chapter 17

ONE OFFICER'S WORST DAY

*The statesman who yields to war fever must realize
that once the signal is given, he is no longer the master of policy
but the slave of unforeseeable and uncontrollable events.*

- Sir Winston Churchill

On July 10 '44, the carrier platoon was detailed to scour the battlefield and search for wounded or dead men of the Rifles. They lay in the tall grain and were hard to see. At first dawn, we started out. It was apparent that a fair number of our troops had been killed in the skirmishes leading to Carpiquet and, later, in the taking of Caen.

At the transport lines, orders were issued that the canvas scaffolding be taken off a 60-hundredweight vehicle, also that palliasses (straw mattresses) be placed on the floor. The truck was guided so that we could carefully pick up the dead and particularly make comfortable the wounded.

The real story lies in the helmet and boots. The RWR who were in the first wave of the D-Day landing were issued Mercury helmets. They had a distinct shape named after the god Mercury. Reinforcements who came later were not issued these helmets. Similarily, the assault troops who went ashore first on Juno Beach wore combat boots which, when laced, were halfway up the calf. They had a pocket sewn in the right side to carry a sheath knife.

The fields were searched carefully. It was July and the crops were coming up in France. We began to notice that a large number of the dead or dying included those who had landed first on the beach and were accorded the accolade of original D-Day veterans. They had survived the landing and the slaughter at Putot-en-Bessin. They lived to fight another day as they advanced across the fields towards Caen. Many of the first ashore died a month later in the battle for Caen.

For the first time, the enormity of what could be seen on that battlefield hit me. Most of these men had enlisted when I had, back in 1940. There was no greater group of guys – loyal, dedicated, proud to be Little Black Devils.

When I looked at the boots and the helmets, I knew without glancing at the shoulder flash that, in all likelihood, I would know the dead or the dying personally. Some new reinforcements had come up with the truck. They were asked to tenderly load these representatives of the greatest generation that ever lived onto a 60-hundredweight truck and take them back for a decent burial, or, for the few who were still alive, to the nearest Casualty Clearing Station (CCS).

I had a sergeant copy down the names. It was not until I sat down to write this memoir 60 years later that I found the nerve to look at the diary and check who they were. Here is a list:

- **RFN LEONARD MILLER** died July 5 '44 at the age of 26. Commemorated by the naming of *Miller Creek* (64 A/5), which flows southwest into Warnews River.

- **RFN JOHN MACK** died July 9 '44 at the age of 20. *Mack Island* (64 G/12) in Big Sand Lake bears his name.

- **RFN ED HEINRICHS** died July 5 '44 at the age of 19. A sad thought came to me after I wrote to his parents. I still have a copy of the letter. Here is one quote: "He loved to read and as to what he planned for the future is hard to say with the war going on. He loved life and his friends." *Heinrichs Lake* (64 N/4) southwest of Nueltin Lake was named after him.

- **LANCE CPL ROBERT MOENAERT** of St. Boniface (across the river from Winnipeg) died July 4 '44 at the age of 21. *Moenaert Lake* (64 K/14), north of Lac Brochet, carries his name.

- **LANCE CPL JOSEPH DONAT PILOTE** of The Pas, Manitoba, died July 4 '44 at the age of 30. *Pilote Lake* (64 C/9), southeast of Reindeer Lake, was named after him by the Manitoba Government.

- **Lance Cpl Steven Popaden** of Winnipegosis died July 5 '44 at the age of 27. He is commemorated by the naming of *Popaden Lake* (64 0/10), northwest of Nejanilini Lake.

- **Rfn James Pulver** of Hamiota, Manitoba, died July 4 '44 at the age of 19. *Pulver Lake* (63 0/4), north of Wekusko Lake, is named after him.

- **Rfn Thomas Troughton** was a strapping young farm worker. On his attestation paper, he said he loved music and drawing. He was killed on July 4 ' 44 at the age of 25. *Troughton Lake* (64 K/8), northeast of Reindeer Lake, carries his name.

AUTHOR'S NOTE: Caen is not on the battle honours for the RWRs. The objective was primarily left to the 9th Brigade with the Stormont, Dundas and Glengarry Highlanders in the lead, along with the Highland Light Infantry from Gault and the North Nova Scotia Highlanders.

From the Government list, however, it is obvious that the battle for Caen saw the end for many of those RWR who landed on D-Day, and who escaped the horror of the slaughter at Putot on the 8th of June.

The book <u>Victory at Falaise: The Soldiers' Story</u> (Harper Collins, 2000) by Denis and Shelagh Whitaker quotes me as follows:

> "Normandy will always be a blur to me. Dust, heat and worst of all the dead guys. I only look at their boots. I do not want to see the RWR shoulder flash or the face. Having been with the battalion since the start, I might know the guy too well." (p. 101)

Perhaps the depth of my emotions lies in the fact that I was an original soldier with the unit. Seeing so many of those whom I knew personally lying dead in the wheat fields of Normandy was a shocker. The combat boots and the Mercury helmet, in all probability, would identify the men who were with us from the first days of the Regiment's mobilization in 1940. I could not bear to see and recognize the crumpled remains of so many brave soldiers.

Canadian infantry walking through ruins at Caen, France 10 July 1944
Courtesy of the National Archives of Canada (PA-162651)

Chapter 18

THE KNIGHTS OF BATTLE IN NORMANDY*

Leadership is the practical application of character

- Colonel R. Meinertzhagen

HARRY KNOX controlled a large area of Normandy as a Company Commander.

When first I saw **HARRY** in my neighbourhood in Winnipeg, he wore a white smock as he ably served the shoppers in a supermarket. He enlisted in the infantry early in World War II and was eventually posted to the RWR. He quickly rose in the ranks. He was on what is today called a 'fast track.'

By the time the Regiment was in Normandy, he was commanding an infantry company. **HARRY KNOX** was the prototype of 'fellow well met.' He made a rapid transition to officer of field grade rank – a designation for Majors. He looked great in the white smock in his job making jokes with the grocery shoppers. He looked even better in a camouflage battle smock, with his tin hat slung over a shoulder and a map case sticking out of a pocket. In the meantime he learned the hard way how to command an infantry company of eager young soldiers.

We met up in a 'hot zone' half way between Caen and Falaise, where today some 5,000 Canadians lie in peace. He had come clipping along the road in a jeep, complete with a tall aerial and a powerful radio set. He had just been through a fierce battle with the German SS. We stopped in a safe farmyard and had a chat. Harry had all the skills of an infantry company commander.

The Dean of Canadian War Correspondents, *ROSS MUNRO* of The Canadian Press (my pre-war boss in Winnipeg) joined the discussion. **HARRY** was enthusiastic about a recent, highly successful attack. He pointed to a concealed copse about 500 yards ahead, stating that, with the

---

* The RWR had a full complement of superior company commanders. Notables include Fred Allen, Norm Wilson-Smith; Dave Campbell …

flick of a radio button, he could give an order to the Forward Observation Officer (FOO) of the Field Artillery for a 25-pounder shoot, or give a command to the lethal 105mm guns mounted on tracked vehicles, also we had our own 3" mortars and mobile anti-tank guns. Sherman tanks, too, were at his 'beck and call.' The German position would be badly shaken.

ROSS MUNRO – always the reporter – got out his notebook, asking for further details. **HARRY**, without a hint of braggadocio, pointed to the sky. He told us that by communication with the Air Liaison Officer (ALO) at Tactical Headquarters, he could bring in the 'Tiffie' fighter bombers with tons of high explosive, smoke bombs or rockets. From his command post (usually a well-concealed jeep), armed with radio communication, **HARRY** could give commands which would bring the entire Division's artillery weapons into play. Another aspect of his ability to dominate the area would be counter-battery fire. He could accurately determine the German gun positions by spotting enemy muzzle flashes. This included the pride of the German artillery – the mobile .88s. Once discovered, they would either be obliterated or have to find another appropriate gun position.

HARRY KNOX wasn't finished. He had been tasked by the CO and was literally in command from his jeep of the coming brigade attack on the town of Renesmesnil, on the route to Falaise.

With this awesome command of firepower, the infantry commander from a farmyard or ditch, had control. If they attacked an objective, his men, with grenades, 303 rifles, and access to Bren and Sten guns, could advance behind an artillery and smoke barrage. The German command post could be annihilated.

This was later ably demonstrated in the attack on Renesmesnil which opened the way to the pivotable 'strong point' of Bretteville-le-Rabet and was reported in the Canadian newspapers by the legendary **ROSS MUNRO**. As **ROSS** put it – the infantry was still the Queen of Battle but had unbelievable help from supporting arms. The story was repeated in the *Maple Leaf* – the army newspaper in Europe. The boys of the RWR understood that, with these tactics, we could dominate the battlefield.

The well-trained majors, while commanding infantry companies, had literal mastery of Normandy from Caen to Falaise - 25 miles in length and 15 miles wide. One legendary Company Commander was **MAJ LOCKIE**

FULTON. Another was **JAKE CARVELL** who started as a signal officer but had decided to fight the war as an infantry company commander. **JAKE** was not satisfied merely to send signals, he wanted to play a close combat role.

HARRY KNOX'S company that morning had been in a tactical manoeuvre with devastating results for the enemy. The ground troops, who otherwise would have had to put in a hand-to-hand bayonet assault, talked of their faith in artillery, tanks and aircraft. Also they acknowledged **KNOX'S** brilliant work as conductor of the assault.

Who else was a Knight of Battle?

PHIL GOWER, on D-Day June 6 '44, earned a reputation beyond belief with his handling of the giant casements at the mouth of the Seulles River where it joins the channel. This constituted one of the major objectives of any of the assault forces in the Normandy landing.

PHIL had an interesting career. He was a Corporal in the Permanent Force prior to the war. After he obtained his commission he came to the RWR and soon showed that he had a thorough grasp of infantry tactics. He knew, also, how to get the best out of his men.

In the Regiment **PHIL** had originally been the second-in-command (2 I/C) of BAKER Company. His looming objective on D-Day was a huge German bunker. The scene was destined to send shivers up the spine of any infantryman. It provided defence, either from the sea or in an outflanking manoeuvre from the rear. Several weeks before the final plans for D-Day, the major originally tasked to command B Company took a staff position at a Headquarters (HQ). This meant that **CO JOHN MELDRAM** had either to bring in a new major or leave this all-important position to **PHIL GOWER**, the 2 I/C – a captain who knew the men and was immensely qualified to organize and carry out the attack. It was a wise decision.

PHIL GOWER was given his normal compliment of 130 men with another 30 or so special combat troops, including engineers and explosive experts. **PHIL'S** landing craft infantry (LCI) came under withering fire. According to the regiment's history, however, the highly-touted support from planes, warships and rockets fired from landing craft failed 'to make one hit on this objective.' (RWR Combat Report)

Of the 160 men – the figure is approximate – who landed with B Company, only 27 survivors could be counted at the end of the day. Many spoke of the heroism of **PHIL GOWER**, standing knee-deep in water. He had taken off his helmet and was using both arms to wave his troops ashore, completely ignoring the German small-arms firing at him. He received a Military Cross for his bravery; a very rare decoration for a company commander holding a captain's rank.

Here the story is scarcely believable. **PHIL** was taken prisoner. Until the end of the war he was in a POW camp, being paid as a Captain although his task would certainly have called for a Major's rank. It gets even worse. After the war, **PHIL** decided to return to the Permanent Force. The policy at that time for officers, staying in the Active Force, was to drop one rank. **PHIL** had been a Captain, hence had to revert to Lieutenant when he joined the Peacetime Army. It was my great fortune to spend a great deal of time with he and his wife Anne, in Ottawa, until he was posted to Calgary and then Korea.

He eventually got his Major's rank - without back pay. Unusually tragic circumstances continued to dog him and he was killed in an Air Canada plane, on Mount Slesse in the Rockies, on his return to Calgary from the Korean War.

Going down the list, it can be suggested that our Company Commanders were as good as any in the U.S. or British Forces. That includes the commandos who landed on D-Day on the immediate left of our 8th Brigade at Saint Aubin. Some of these 'Knights of the Battlefield,' and the list is by no means complete, would include **MAJORS FRED HODGE**, **HUGH DENISON**, and **BRIAN ROBERTSON** - all killed in action.

The point being made: A company commander had, at his fingertips, an almost unlimited number of 25-pounders; anti-tank guns if needed for defence; air support from what was known as the 'cab ranks' of close-support aircraft flying above the battle and always ready for action, and even some of the 'funnies,' such as the Crocodile flamethrower tanks. The so-called 'funnies' were the product of the ingenious mind of **SIR PERCY HOBART** – the father of the floating Sherman tanks which were effective on D-Day.

British Crocodile Tank

Crocodile flamethrowers were usually mounted on Churchill tanks. Petards were a tank which could rush up to a German fortification, plant a beehive charge consisting of thousands of pounds of TNT against a wall, back off and open a breach from which the infantry could penetrate.

Where did the Canadian Army find field commanders such as **HARRY KNOX**? Their German counterparts were trained in infantry, tank or tactical schools – not so our Company commanders. They simply joined the Forces and used their natural ability to pick up the finer points of their jobs. It is remarkable that such officers had command of a battlefield many miles long and wide.

Our Infantry Battalions, or individual companies, using the supporting arms as necessary, wiped out or subdued the well prepared German positions. The German commanders – mostly in mobile vehicles – were perplexed about the courage and the knowledge of these new commanders of the battlefield.

Some say our victory in Normandy was a 'fluke.' Who won? Who lost?

Chapter 19

THE YOUNG TURKS

*Older men declare war. But it's the youth
who must fight and die!*

- Herbert Hoover

In a memoir of this type, it is impossible to note every Winnipeg Rifle who earned the recognition of his fellow soldiers, his home community and his country. A few will give the picture of the platoon leaders who were responsible for much of the respect in which the Little Black Devils were held.

The company commanders (mostly majors) were in charge of the battle stretching over thousands of acres of Normandy from Juno Beach to the city of Caen on the east, the axis of the railway and major highway on the south, and the in-and-out border with the British on the right of the battle zone. Another factor of battle is the part played by Non-Commissioned Officers (NCOs).

It was, however, the young, well-disciplined, well-trained subalterns (lieutenants) who acted as the liaison between the majors (literally the brains – no kidding) and the hard-hitting NCOs. The story of some of the lieutenants who, most in their early 20's, lost their lives in Normandy is heroic beyond belief.

The wastage (the official term, not mine) of lieutenant platoon commanders in the infantry was pitifully high. In our own battalion by October 10 '44, the odds were: Out of every ten subalterns in the combat companies, three would be killed and seven would be put out of action by severe wounds; none would survive unharmed.

LT DENNIS BENNETT, a bright former company clerk was sent to qualify for OCTU (Officer Cadet Training Unit). He returned to the battalion about mid-August. He was detailed to attend a platoon commander course being held during a quiet period. I had known **DENNIS** from the day he joined the battalion early in the war. He had not taken long to shed the personification of an administrator, and had become a first-rate combat officer.

He was sent on a fighting patrol on September 14 '44 and was killed returning to his Platoon Headquarters. It was a very confused situation, with machine guns firing from both the RWR and the desperate Jerries. When the remnants of the patrol were returning, there was a mix-up in the password (Defenders were to say "Mistletoe", and the returning patrol was to answer "New Years").

The CO conducted a quick but intense investigation. The official description of **DENNIS'** death was: "Cut down by bullets in No Man's Land while returning from a reconnaissance into the German lines."

A sad ending for a great young officer. **DENNIS** is buried in Calais War Cemetery. The geographical feature named after him by the Manitoba Government is *Bennett Bay* (64 I/10) in North West Manitoba.

Another courageous lieutenant, who had been a schoolteacher in Cornwall, Ontario, came up to us as a reinforcement at the Leopold Canal on October 7 '44. His name was **GERRY LEMAY**. He was hit by mortar fire the second night. He survived, but left a leg behind in the canal bank. He died years later of what was called 'his pensionable disability.' His name is included in this section, firstly, to pay tribute to his courage and, secondly, to indicate how brief the period of combat for young officers could be.

Another sad loss for the Regiment was **LT ROLAND (RON) DONOGH**. He died July 19 '44 at the age of 22 and is buried in Bretteville-sur-Laize Cemetery. He was the eldest son of the Reverend Wallace R. and Mabel Donogh of Glenboro, Manitoba. **RON** was a brilliant student at the University of Manitoba. He was known, also, as a first-rate athlete and a good musician. The geographical feature named after him by the Manitoba Government is *Donogh Island* (63 J/13) in Wekusko Lake.

There has always been some controversy, but it was believed at the time (although this can never be proved) that **RON** was hit by a shell from one of our own artillery pieces in the rear. His younger brother, **NORM DONOGH**, was also in the RWRs. **NORM** was wounded but survived the war to become the Honorary Lieutenant Colonel of the Regiment in the post-war militia.

Another of the 'Young Turks' who came to the Regiment from the ranks was **Lt Doug Kirkpatrick**. He died on August 28 '44 – and how well and sadly the circumstances were known to me. He was in Charlie Company, of which I happened to be the commanding officer. It happened just after we crossed the Seine River at Elbeuf. We saw some activity in a hedgerow about 400 yards to our right. It was my responsibility to call up the mobile artillery – the 105mm mounted on tanks – to give covering fire.

Doug Kirkpatrick orchestrated the operation, bringing the 105s in from a roadway just west of the German position. He was last seen leading the attack, in which the RWR was successful. **Doug's** signaller sent back a sad message. **Doug** was badly wounded and probably would not live.

By the time I reached the scene, **Doug**, at the age of 25, was dead.

He was, in pre-war times, a popular employee of the T. Eaton Company in Winnipeg. **Doug** graduated from Gordon Bell High School in Winnipeg. He took accountancy at night school and was well on his way to making a career for himself. **Doug** was the son of John and Dora Kirkpatrick, and was married to Ella Kirkpatrick of Toronto. He left a wife and a daughter, as well as his grieving parents.

Doug is commemorated by the naming of *Kirkpatrick Lake* (64 I/9), northeast of North Knife Lake, in far northern Manitoba. Such was the camaraderie between lieutenants like **Doug** and myself that, for 60 years, I have laid a separate wreath at the War Memorial in honour of both **Doug Kirkpatrick** and **Lew McQueen**, mentioned earlier as having been killed at the battle of Putot.

The 'Wee Scotsman'

The battle ground is a very strange place; and it is certainly not unusual to witness unforgettable events.

It may not be generally known but in the ranks of the infantry, the band members are generally the stretcher-bearers, when not playing instruments.

JIMMY BULLOCH, a well-known Winnipeg athlete before he was a Sergeant and then Lieutenant with the RWRs, came up to me in a jeep and said that we should go and get **DOUG KIRKPATRICK** who was lying wounded in a hedge row. We had all been great, great friends in the battalion and during our training. There was no need for any urging.

DOUG was hit about an hour before dusk. Several attempts to get to him, as he was 20 or 30 yards ahead of his platoon at the hedge row, were unsuccessful. The Canadian Scottish Regiment (CanScots) had an excellent pipe band. Their pipers did yomen service as stretcher-bearers but many of them carried their pipes with them on the stretchers.

This is what happened. A piper that we still today call 'WEE JAMIE' came out of the mist from the area held by the CanScots. He was wearing a kilt and playing his bagpipes. He was taking a tremendous chance because the Germans, in retreat, were ferocious. Why, then, did they stop firing when they saw this short-statured soldier with his bagpipes and his kilt heading straight for the area where several wounded RWRs (including **DOUG KIRKPATRICK**) were lying? Some would say they were mesmerized. I would think that it showed that even in the most ferocious soldier lies a spark of human decency. In any event, with the twilight, the strains of *Fleurs of the Forest* and the obvious courage by 'WEE JAMIE' stilled the MGs of the Germans long enough for us to go out with the jeep and bring **DOUG** and another RWR back – then the episode was over.

I knew a number of the officers of the CanScots. Later I approached Platoon Commander **RALPH COSIER** and asked him to find out who 'WEE JAMIE' was. He went back to the area where the band was dug in, borrowed a motorcycle and came back and said: "There are four really short pipers who could have fit the description. None of them would own up to this outstanding act of valour." We shall never know who he was but if he reads this book, please write to me. I have a letter from Ella, **DOUG KIRKPATRICK'S** wife, that he should have.

An extraordinary situation developed in regard to the death of **LT GEORGE McKINNON**, another NCO who was commissioned from the ranks. He died on August 19 '44 while engaged in a hair-raising battle. He was in an 800-weight vehicle (just larger than a jeep) when accosted by a German M4 tank. The odds were too great. He is commemorated by the naming of *McKinnon Island* (64 F/7) in Wells Lake in northern Manitoba.

On a pilgrimage to Normandy in 1995, I met **JACK TENNANT**, a nephew of **GEORGE MCKINNON**. **JACK** was covering the pilgrimage for the *Calgary Herald*. I was able to show the reporter **GEORGE'S** grave and fill him in on the manner in which his uncle had been killed. The reporter told me that he was an eight-year-old Manitoba farm boy when he heard of the death of his uncle. He said that it was the saddest day in the farming community of Arrow River when **GEORGE'S** wife received the standard telegram which commenced, "The government regrets to inform you..."

In writing this memoir, **GEORGE'S** nephew, **JACK**, caught up with me. Although I knew **GEORGE** well, I was able to get even more details. He told me that, when **GEORGE** was on his leave, to keep in good physical shape he would run about three miles, and would polish his brass, boots and Sam Browne belt every day. As his nephew said: "I followed him about like a wee puppy because he was everything I ever wanted to be. Then he was gone – forever."

LT DON RIESBERRY was a promising graduate of Brandon University. He was killed on October 11 '44, in the infamous battle of the Leopold Canal. **DON** had gone overseas with the Royal Saskatchewan Regiment, later transferring to the RWRs. His widow, living in Brandon, Manitoba, was visited by a number of RWRs including myself. She showed us some of his trophies, mostly for academic work. In particular, she was proud of the fact that he had studied under the noted Manitoba historian, **DR. W.L. MORTON**. As a personal comment, we should stop and think of the loss to Canada of the brilliant minds possessed by people with this capability. **LT RIESBERRY** is commemorated by the naming of *Riesberry Lake* (64 I/2), east of North Knife Lake in Manitoba.

LT GLEN STEWART of Austin, Manitoba died at the age of 30 on July 4 '44. He was the son of John and Elizabeth Stewart and was survived by his wife Wilhelmina Stewart of Austin, Manitoba. He was raised in Portage la Prairie, a middle-sized city about 50 miles west of Winnipeg. His widow wrote and stated how proud he was to have won the Governor General's Medal upon graduation as a pharmacist. Again, a comment begs to be included: the 'Young Turks' did more than their share of the fighting and commanding of the RWRs in Normandy. It is sad, however, to think of the loss to Canada. **LT STEWART** is commemorated by the naming of *Stewart Peninsula* (63 N/2) on Limestone Point Lake in Manitoba.

In searching the records, it is noted that **GLEN** was killed in a mortar attack by one of the most dangerous weapons the Germans had – the Nebelwerfer or six-barrelled mortar. In the air the shells made a noise like a boxcar. The troops christened them Moaning Minnies.

LT JOHN W. BENHAM of Winnipeg is mentioned earlier in regard to the battle at Putot. He died June 8 '44 at the age of 31 and is buried at Bretteville-sur-Laize Canadian War Cemetery. He was the son of Alfred W. and Grace M. Benham of Winnipeg and was survived by his wife Millicent Benham. *Benham Lake* (64 N/12), southwest of Nueltin Lake was named after him in 1972. He saw only two days of action - but his gallantry is the stuff of legends.

LT RICHARD E. CHRISTMAS of Winnipeg. A proud RWR, he was MENTIONED IN DISPATCHES. He died June 6 '44 at the age of 27 - the only RWR officer killed at Juno Beach. He is commemorated at Beny-sur-Mer Canadian War Cemetery, France. He was the son of Herbert and Mabel Christmas. According to his nephew:

"He was educated at Lord Roberts School and St. John's College in Winnipeg. He was active in Boy Scouts and was a member of St. Alban's Anglican Church. Before joining the army, he was employed with the British North America Insurance company. Had he survived the war, he contemplated a career in the church or the insurance industry. He joined the RWR in 1940. My uncle received his commission of 2nd Lieutenant on August 12, 1940. He went overseas with the battalion in July, 1942 and for one year acted as instructor in a battle course. On March 22, 1945 he was mentioned in a dispatch for distinguished service. He was wounded in action on Normandy Beach on June 6, 1944 and died later from his wounds."

Christmas Lake (54 K/12), east of Churchill was named after him in 1948.

LT JOHN ESARUK of Stony Mountain died September 25 '44 at the age of 27. His remains were laid to rest at Calais Canadian War Cemetery in France. He was the son of Alex and Irene Esaruk of Winnipeg and was survived by his wife Doris I. Esaruk (née Newman) and their son. He had seen his son only once and only for a few hours before his departure overseas. **LT ESARUK** had joined the Princess Patricia's Canadian Light

Infantry in 1937 and worked his way through the ranks to earn a commission in 1941. He was held back in England as an instructor but was so eager to get to France that he transferred to the RWRs.

JOHN was proud of telling the story of how he was picked up by the Provost while on leave in Truro, Nova Scotia. The charge was that he was improperly dressed, having removed his badges and insignia of rank. The Canadian Provost telephoned the RWR orderly officer, which happened to be me. This conversation took place:

CHADDERTON:	"Orderly officer here."
PROVOST CORPS:	"This is Corporal John [?] of the Canadian Provost Corps. May I enquire as to your rank?"
CHADDERTON:	"Brigadier, the last time I looked" (in a joking voice).
PROVOST CORPS:	"You have an officer with the rank of lieutenant by the name of John Esaruk?"
CHADDERTON:	"Yes indeed, and a first-class officer he is."
PROVOST CORPS:	"We have to charge him with conduct to the prejudice of good order and military discipline."

He went on to say that John had been picked up in a public place, having removed his badges of rank.

CHADDERTON:	"That sounds like our John. Out on the town for a night with the boys. I am happy to put in a good word for him. We'll need him soon enough."

He was given a reprimand. He would be proud and happy to know that his escapade is on record with the Canadian Archives (the source for this anecdote). *Esaruk Lake* (64 K/12), northeast of Reindeer Lake was named after him in 1972.

LT HENRY J. GROSS of Winnipeg was a first class subaltern with the RWR. **HANK** died September 13 '44 at the age of 26. He was killed by a German sniper while on a recce patrol looking for an entrance to Calais. His men made a stretcher from an old door. They were in tears as they brought him to the RAP. He was laid to rest in the Calais Canadian War Cemetery in France. He was the son of Joseph F. and Barbara Gross and was survived by his wife Margaret. *Gross Island* (53 L/2) in Muche Lake was named after him in 1995.

LT JAMES C. KERR of St. Vital, Manitoba. He was commissioned from the ranks and returned to the RWRs. **JIM** died October 10 '44 at the age of 22 and is buried at Adegem Canadian War Cemetery, Maldegem, Oost-Vlaanderen, Belgium. He was the only son of Colin A. and Hilda H. Kerr and was survived by his wife Alice of Yarmouth, Nova Scotia. His sister writes:

"He was a very friendly, outgoing young man and enjoyed many sports activities including lawn bowling. He was also an avid bridge player. Jim was a very kind and thoughtful person and I have been reading some of his letters sent to me and my parents that showed his deep love for his family. He was married to Alice, a lovely girl from Nova Scotia. Recently, we wrote for and received a tape in which Cliff Chadderton mentioned Jim and told of a visit to my parents' home after Jim's death and spoke of the closeness of the family.

We have just received a video tape titled The Ballad of Jimmy Kerr. Cliff Chadderton had a friend write a song and he asked that it be titled The Ballad of Jimmy Kerr. We were very moved by it."

Kerr Island (64 F/1) in Melvin Lake was named after him in 1995.

LT KENNETH P. PRITCHARD of Winnipeg died February 21 '45 at the age of 21 and is commemorated at the Groesbeek Canadian War Cemetery in Holland. He was the son of Russell M. and Gladys E. Pritchard of Winnipeg. *Pritchard Point* (64 N/16) on Nahili Lake was named after him in 1995.

LT LEWIS J. MCQUEEN of St. James, Manitoba joined the RWR as a private soldier. Later he earned his commission. His bravery is set out earlier in this memoir for actions in the battle of Putot. He died on June 8 '44, on his 24th birthday. He is buried at Beny-sur-Mer. **LEW** was the second son of Heber and Gladys McQueen. He is survived by his wife Iona. His brother **GORDON** also served in the RWRs but was not killed. He wrote of his younger brother **LEW**, as follows:

"Upon leaving school he worked for Schumacher-MacKenzie Ltd, electrical contractors at 334 Main Street, Winnipeg. [He] joined the Royal Winnipeg Rifles in June, 1940. By early 1941, he had risen to the rank of Sergeant. While in England, he was recommended for a commission and was accepted. He returned to Canada and got his commission early in 1943.

Lew returned to England to a holding unit. Several weeks before D-Day, he rejoined the RWR. Lew went in with his platoon with the first wave on D-Day. He was killed in action … at Putot-en-Bessin. He was later found on the south side of the Caen - Bayeux railway."

McQueen Lake (54 K/12), southeast of Churchill was named after him in 1948. His brother erected a plaque at the lake in 1988.

SGT BOB GRAY of Lundar died June 8 '44 at the age of 36 and is buried in Bretteville-sur-Laize Canadian War Cemetery in Calvados, France. He was the son of Robert and Pearl Gray and was survived by his wife Hilda of Winnipeg. He was killed by the German SS in the mass murder after Putot. *Gray Peninsula* (64 K/16) on Burnie Lake was named after him in 1995.

CPL JAMES HENRY of Brandon died August 15 '44 at the age of 27 and is commemorated at Bretteville-sur-Laize Canadian War Cemetery in Calvados, France. He was the son of Joseph E. and Margaret M. Henry (née Jones) of Brandon and was survived by a wife, Margie, and their daughter. She writes:

"When my mother received news of my father, I was one year old. Like many children of war victims, I never knew him. The only knowledge came from family, friends and pictures of his early life. Their memories of him showed me he was a compassionate and caring person who had everyone's interest at heart. This proved true to me a few years ago after being located by a long distance call from an old veteran who served with him. He had been reminiscing about the war and how fortunate he was to be alive thanks to my father who pushed him in a fox hole. Others weren't as fortunate.

In 1956, I had the good fortune to visit his grave in France. This provided a bond that was not there before."

Henry Island (64 N/6) in Burch Lake was named after him in 1995.

LT MORRIS M. SORONOW should, in my opinion, be awarded the highest possible decoration for devotion and for pure, simple desire. **MORRIS** came to Charlie Company in August '44. He was a brilliant lawyer and up until that time had been employed with the Judge Advocate General staff. He was Jewish, however, and felt that he should serve in a capacity which would put him face-to-face with the Germans who had killed more than 6,000 of his religious faith. It was my sad duty to lay out a plan which saw **MORRIS** lead a platoon of Charlie Company more or less in a wild bayonet charge. He was given covering fire, from a copse on the right, by another platoon under **JIM BULLOCK**, a former sergeant who was one of the 'Young Turks.'

We had called for smoke and covering fire on the German position, but a more important target had come up on the road to Reims involving an attack by **DOUG KIRKPATRICK**. Through the little 18-set, I ordered **MORRIS** to turn back, and his last words to me were, "If there are Germans in that farmhouse, I'm going to kill every one of them." Seconds later, he was hit by machine gun bullets, and his war was over.

LT SORONOW died August 28 '44 at the age of 33 and is buried at the Calais Canadian War Cemetery in France. *Soronow Lake* (64 K/5), south of Lac Brochet, was named after him in 1972.

Chapter 20

JEDEDIAH'S CREED

'One son for the soil, And one son for the sea.'

When Agnes Morgan's two sons left to join the services in World War II (**JIM** was enlisting in the Army; **JACK** was heading for the Naval Recruiting Station), she repeated the Jedediah Creed, noted above.

When **JIM MORGAN**, a rifleman with the RWR, was being given the Last Rites by **PADRE EDWARD HORTON** after sustaining serious wounds in the Battle for Bretteville-le-Rabet, he was heard to repeat the words to the **PADRE** and to his comrades – "I'm the son for the soil."

When *Morgan Point* on Chartrand Lake (64 K/1) was being named in honour of **JIM**, his wife, Olga wrote "I have letters from the **PADRE** of his regiment during the Invasion and he spoke very highly of **JIM**. He had had many talks."

RFN MORGAN died June 16 '44 at the age of 34 and is buried at Beny-sur-Mer Canadian War Cemetery in France. He was the son of James and Agnes Morgan and was survived by his wife Olga of Winnipeg.

Chapter 21

GOD AND WAR

Rolling and rolling there
Where God seems not to care;
Till the fierce Love they bear
Cramps them in death's extreme decrepitude.

Wilfrid Owen

A CHRISTIAN BURIAL

We were resting after a scouting mission around the walls of the Abbaye d'Ardenne. There was a large gate at the north end of the Abbaye but it was locked. It was July 10 '44.

We proceeded along the Eastern wall to a smaller gate which was partly open. **LEN SYLVESTER**, who came from a small town in Saskatchewan, was one of our best Bren Gunners. This gate was an opportunity for the Germans to get into and out of the Abbaye. **LEN** was left behind to guard it. We continued in a southerly direction along the road that ran outside of the stone wall of the Abbaye. To circle the entire enclosure took about one-half hour. On the way back, the plan was to pick up **LEN SYLVESTER**. The minute we saw him we knew he had been killed, probably from a sniper in the fields east of the Abbaye. His body was carefully hauled into the carrier and we proceeded around the southern wall. Bodies of two other RWRs and a Regina Rifle were waiting to be buried. Alongside of them were two dead German Wehrmacht lying on their backs. Their full grey green jackets were unbuttoned.

In the meantime a message had been sent to **PADRE EDWARD HORTON**. He showed up with his jeep, complete with shovels. We dug the graves, then turned the entire business over to the Padre.

He made it clear that this would be a Christian burial for both the Canadians and the Germans. Some RWRs demurred. The **PADRE** quelled any doubts with a withering look and then proceeded with an emotional ceremony. It was quiet, the sun was shining; birds were chirping.

Before the bodies were committed to the ground, **LORNE CAMERON**, a stretcher-bearer from British Columbia, was obviously overcome. With tears in his eyes, and shaking his head, he asked **PADRE HORTON** how God could allow all this killing. The **PADRE** hated to see men die, whether the enemy or our own. He put his arm around Lorne to comfort him.

Lorne used words like God being 'all powerful.' As he sobbed on the **PADRE'S** shoulder, he asked the question that has occurred to many in battle. His exact words were written in my diary. Here they are:

> "I believe in God, but if He is the All Powerful, why does he allow this war and all this killing?"

The **PADRE** swept his arm around to take in the whole battlefield. He hated killing and whenever he was face-to-face with death, it showed on him. One of his main tasks was conducting burial services. The **PADRE** was always left shaken for hours after an ordeal of this sort, but he never let his feelings interfere while doing his job. His services were simple, but gut-wrenching.

The **PADRE** stopped, looked at **LORNE** with a deep frown on his face. He was mulling over the answer. I copied his words in my diary.

> "You ask why God allows this killing. Doesn't it seem reasonable that God can help only those who will help themselves? If there are certain people who will not co-operate then naturally evil will arise. If everyone obeyed God's laws there COULD NOT be evil in the world."

The **PADRE** had made his point ... rather beautifully, we thought.

He then reminded the Canadians that we held regular church parades - and that the Germans did likewise. God was all-knowing. The Heavenly Father, under whose guidance we lived, was no doubt watching.

The **PADRE** pointed to the German soldiers, noting that they wore belt buckles inscribed with GOTT MITT UNS (GOD IS WITH US). Some may argue that under **HITLER** the power of the church was diminished. The **PADRE** pointed out that so long as a German was willing to wear a belt buckle with the inscription GOTT MITT UNS, he was recognizing a supreme being, higher than his own Fuhrer. My Mother would have said: "In his house there are many mansions." LORNE knelt beside one of the Germans and patted his shoulder in a gesture of sorrow. The setting belied the terrible circumstances.

The PADRE had a way of lifting our spirits and in a clear voice he said: "If you know this hymn, sing it with me."

> What a friend we have in Jesus
> All our sins and griefs to bear
> What a privilege to carry
> Everything to God in prayer

The song carried over the battlefield on this quiet evening!

Chaplains aid in the evacuation of wounded soldiers at Caen, France 15 July 1944.
Courtesy of the National Archives of Canada (PA-133244)

Chapter 22

EARL MCINTYRE AND THE MORTAL SIN OF KILLING

Now, God be thanked Who has matched us with His hour,
And caught our youth, and wakened us from sleeping,
With hand made sure, clear eye and sharpened power,
To turn, as swimmers into cleanness leaping,
Glad from a world grown old and cold and weary . . .

Rupert Brooke

One of the most unusual cases involving religion occurred after the RWR battle at Cormelles, south of Caen. **EARL MCINTYRE** was a stalwart Christian. He did volunteer work with the United Protestant Church in the Morden, Manitoba area prior to enlistment. In a written account for the Morden newspaper, he described an almost overpowering resistance to enlistment. He spoke of his revulsion at thinking that he might have to kill another human being.

Notwithstanding, he showed unusual courage at the fierce fighting around the Abbaye d'Ardenne (July '44). After the loss of two of his close friends, we spoke as we looked for a safe place to re-group.

He warned that he had studied the principles followed by the conscientious objectors – those whose beliefs would not allow them to carry arms. He added that he could not see himself spending the rest of his life with the label of a conscientious objector. He saw no quarrel with their right to differ. He was quick to say though, that he could not find himself in agreement with their arguments.

He did suggest that any conscientious objectors to whom he had spoken appeared to be somewhat illogical but he was not critical of their beliefs. **EARL** made it plain that he did not wish to pursue this idea. He then came right to the point.

He was quick to tell me that he was not afraid in the normal sense that we bandied the word around in the infantry. He was, however, having very real trouble accepting that there was any justification strong enough, in him, to kill another human being.

This was a strange twist. By this time, he had given a sterling account of himself in combat. The ability to realize that fear is a natural component of life was not in question. Living with the ever-present circumstances in which a soldier in Normandy faced death – day and night – was even acceptable to him. He could not bring himself to believe, however, that he should be the one doing the killing.

EARL MCINTYRE'S fear was creating for him an entirely different mental impediment. Those of us who knew him well were aware that he was not afraid to die or to be injured. It was his belief, as a true Christian, that his reluctance to kill was the obstacle. His worry was one which would appear to have occurred only to a few, but **EARL** knew he was one of them. His concern was whether he could meet the test. How could he reconcile his acts with the teachings of the Bible, having himself killed other men? In his view, he was committing mortal sins almost on a daily basis.

His circumstances sent my mind into a tailspin. He had spoken to me of his love of God. This had led him to worship the Lord, as he said, "Every day – and in every way."

I let the problem sit for a few moments. Then the thought came to me. Perhaps this was a time for simple philosophy.

Certainly I could not reply to him on theological terms. It was necessary to get practical. I suggested that if he survived the war, he could become a preacher and spend the rest of his life in a form of repentance. He could dedicate himself to helping others.

EARL grabbed my left elbow in his powerful hand and turned so that he looked me straight in the eye. I had given him the answer. My first reaction was disbelief, but then it was evident. **EARL** was looking for some way to carry on. I had given it to him.

In the next weeks of ferocious battle actions, he showed all the attributes of a fearless infantry leader. He was far and away one of the best section commanders we had. Moreover, it was noticeable that he was at peace with himself. **EARL** had been a silent witness to **PADRE HORTON'S** explanation, when we relaxed in a quiet area just outside of the walls of the Abbaye d'Ardenne.

EARL was presumably able to function, notwithstanding his state of mind. He had rationalized that killing was necessary. If God spared him, he had made his own covenant to compensate for his failure to obey the Sixth Commandment.

EARL MCINTYRE and I saw quite a bit of each other later as we spent days patrolling and taking cover from the incessant German shelling. **EARL** had gained a wealth of moral courage. He had been able to overcome his fear by placing his faith in an understanding. His self-imposed pledge was that, if his life were spared, he would enter a post-war vocation in which he would, as he put it, 'get back on the right side of the ledger.'

My relationship with **EARL** was strengthened after his return to Canada. Like me, he found himself in the ranks of the war amputees. He became a staunch advocate for The War Amps NEVER AGAIN! Program. It sanctions military preparedness if necessary, but is dedicated to the hope that man can find a more humane method of settling differences. The Program's theme: 'those who bear the scars of war must do everything to prevent another global conflict.'

EARL and his wife, Anne, raised a wonderful family. **EARL**, my friend and colleague, went to his peaceful rest on March 6 '98. He died with his sins forgiven. Of this I am certain.

Strangely enough, he told me that he abhorred the hymn Onward Christian Soldiers. It was seldom realized, he felt, that 'Christian Soldiers' were being exhorted to fight sin. Yet, as **EARL** saw it, the ordinary soldier, who was without a strong background in religion, might see it as a battle cry to encourage slaughter of other men.

Here is the first verse:

> *Onward, Christian soldiers, marching as to war,*
> *With the cross of Jesus going on before:*
> *Christ the royal Master leads against the foe;*
> *Forward into battle, see, His banner go.*

Chapter 23

BATTLE EXHAUSTION

Just a closer walk with thee
Grant it Jesus is my plea
Daily walking close to thee
Let it be, Dear Lord, let it be

Traditional Hymn

The Canadian General staff had established a system which was intended to deal with soldiers in Normandy who felt they were unable to function under the dangerous and rigorous conditions of combat. The official term ... Battle Exhaustion Centre (BE).

The battalion commanders could, however, develop an option to ignore the medically-oriented group of psychologists and psychiatrists. In some instances, the COs refused to acknowledge even the existence of battle exhaustion. The diagnosis would have been necessary in cases referred for medical treatment at one of these official centres.

The RWR was no exception. It appeared to be a fairly well-kept secret, but B Echelon (the administrative headquarters twice removed from the combat troops) had established its own system of recuperation.

LT COL JOHN MELDRAM, the CO of the RWR, much preferred to use his own creation which was dubbed 'the tent.' This operated (quietly) under the Regimental Medical Officer (MO) and the Regimental Padre.

There was very little talk about battle exhaustion in the forward units of the infantry. If a man really had 'lost it,' the MO would normally be obliged to send him back through regular channels for treatment. The information would have to go on his file. This was uppermost in the minds of many who had volunteered to fight and did not wish to be taken out of action because they appeared to lack courage. In fact, many of them had already lived through the hell of D-Day and a good part of Normandy before they broke down.

As an alternative, some battalion COs established their own system where the soldier who had 'gotten the wind up' could be taken out of action and given a few days' rest and a chance to talk things over with others in the same category. As a result, at any given time, 'the tent' (which was really located under shady trees with picnic benches and, in some cases, a little supply of rum or beer) was the area for recuperation within the unit for what came to be known as battle exhaustion. Incidentally, the term in current use is PTSD - post-traumatic stress disorder. It was a term invented after World War II and few, if any, combat troops were discharged with this on their medical records.

The usual scenario: visits by friends still at unit were encouraged, if combat conditions were quiet. It was brought home that, if he were evacuated as a BE case, reports might get back to his friends and family... with the result that he would be dubbed a 'slacker' (even though his previous combat experience might indicate otherwise). Quite possibly the problem was one of having used up the reservoir of determination and the will to continue in combat. It was thought that where fear had crept in, it could be overcome by reminding the riflemen of a number of factors. First always: pride in the Regiment Esprit de Corps began to mean something tangible. A second suggestion could be that his comrades back at the combat positions needed him.

It was driven home to him that there was no attitude of shame and that he would be accepted back in his platoon, presumably on the basis that he had been subjected to a situation which forced a temporary removal from a combat zone.

There are no reliable reports of statistics, but the system certainly did work.

Many of those who got sent back to 'the tent' voluntarily returned to combat. They were strengthened by their actions in showing that they could 'hack it.' Also, their friends back in the areas of heavy action welcomed them. Quite often his mates did not even know the circumstances.

Back at 'the tent,' a soldier may have strengthened his resolve by speaking with others. Such conversations were often enough to restore the courage to go back and take part in a dangerous and deadly existence.

The unit system of handling battle exhaustion cases does need explanation. It remained unrecognized as part of the battalion's *modus operandi*. The system was put into effect shortly after D-Day and continued until the end of the war. (No reference to the system appears in official War Histories.)

Not all 'front line' regiments used this system. It was a 'buckshee' operation without official clearance. It was felt that it would function better if its existence was not a matter of public knowledge even within the unit. Some officers of other infantry regiments did not know of the existence of this 'homespun' attempt to bolster the flagging determination of some of the best troops. It seemed to work best on a relationship between the man and his fellow soldiers.

The nomenclature 'the tent' implies that the number of troops accorded this treatment was relatively small. Usually not more than seven or eight people would be 'accommodated' at one time. An important point was sometimes overlooked by the professionals – in the middle of the night, soldiers are apt to talk about things that would not be brought out in daylight hours. Hence the strict rule: all slept in one large enclosure.

'Midnight' confessions were therapeutic. If the system failed, the MO could send the soldier back for treatment through official channels.

A note of interest: Those who feel they are 'in the know' regarding battle exhaustion as it occurred in Normandy are quick to categorize the problem as lack of courage. This did happen. There were, however, many other reasons. **LT GLEN HUGHES** exhibited one – he was challenging himself because he could not bear the thought that his lack of experience was getting troops killed. (See next Chapter)

Also, the fighting capability was sometimes diminished by personal factors; for example, the man who could not bear the thought of his grieving mother or fatherless child. Their circumstances were certainly different from the soldier who had no dependents. The unmarried soldier could adopt an attitude described as 'free and easy,' without having to go into action worried about others. Some soldiers who had been raised in Christian families were bothered about killing the enemy, particularly when, after a battle, they viewed at close range a dead 16-year-old enemy soldier.

Combat infantry were taught never to go through the private possessions of a dead German. It might mean looking through a wallet and seeing photographs of fathers, mothers, or young children. This would make it harder to accept the fact that, in a few days, they would again be asked to kill another human being. Even if the German soldier was out to kill him, the Canadian soldier was told to consider the German as a product of Nazi Germany. In other words, a Canadian infantryman who got a little too personal about an enemy he just killed was setting himself up with the extra burden of guilt.

Chapter 24

GLEN HUGHES

"And then he did the bravest thing of all.
He could no longer bear the thought of his men at the front
enduring the miseries from which he had escaped,
and he intimated his willingness to return to duties.
He did return, and was wounded again."

Sigfried Sassoon – Britain's premier WWI poet

The last thoughts of those who gave their lives in the ferocious battles in Normandy died with them. Sometimes, however, there are clues.

LT GLEN W. HUGHES, whose parents were homesteaders in the Grandview and Neepawa districts of Manitoba, was a member of the reinforcement unit of the RWRs, holding the rank of Captain. So anxious was he to join in combat that he reverted to the lower rank of Lieutenant after D-Day. He had seen many of our young officers come back as casualties and had seen reports of those who were killed in action. Therefore, when GLEN HUGHES performed the unselfish act of reverting to Lieutenant, to join the Winnipeg Rifles during the dirtiest part of the Normandy campaign, it was the bravest thing of all.

When he joined the Rifles in Normandy after the battle of Caen, he ran into many in the unit who knew him well. He had been employed as a Phys. Ed. Teacher at Kelvin High School in the Fort Rouge and River Heights districts of Winnipeg. He knew many of the Rifles and, more to the point, many of them knew him.

On joining the Regiment, he was given an infantry platoon. Although he had little or no opportunity to gain combat experience, he was a good leader and his men looked up to him. This was not too difficult. His six-foot athletic frame and his commanding bearing were indications that his platoon was in good hands.

The battle conditions in a number of actions south of Caen were fierce. As I knew **GLEN HUGHES** personally, some of his platoon gratuitously offered comments about his courage and his leadership.

After distinguishing himself in the battle, he exhibited another trait of a real hero. He consulted with the CO, **LT COL JOHN MELDRAM**, saying that he wondered if he really was fit to command troops in action. The CO asked me to sit in as I had known Glen, in fact, had played basketball for his High School Team.

He could not be certain and did not want to take the responsibility if his inexperience in action could cause the death of eager young riflemen.

Some who did not know **GLEN** might mistakenly conclude that he, himself, was suffering battle exhaustion. Nothing could be further from the truth. He had been a teacher at a prominent high school in Winnipeg. He was quite accustomed to showing leadership. He wondered if the CO had some magic formula for measuring the battle readiness of his officers. **JOHN MELDRAM** was quick to realize that **HUGHES**, a well-known Winnipegger, should never be sent back through the medical chain of command. The danger of being pegged as lacking courage was only too real. This could represent a burden which would follow him after he returned to 'Civvy Street.'

He was the perfect candidate for the Regiment's system of dealing with situations of this nature. In this case it could not be called battle exhaustion. Rather, the situation would best be described as 'love' for his fellow man.

When **SIR DOUGLAS BADER** described men who had lost their lives in action as being 'all heroes,' he would undoubtedly include officers like **GLEN HUGHES**. He had reverted from Captain – a cushy job in the Reinforcement unit – to get into action. This in itself requires a certain type of intestinal fortitude.

When he consulted the CO, he was not out to 'save his own skin,' as they say. He just wondered whether he was to blame for some of the casualties, as he had very little training as a combat officer. At that particular time, the average life span in action of an infantry subaltern could be measured, not in weeks, but in days. **GLEN** knew all of this. With his volitional action, which brought him face to face with the merciless troops of the Hitler Jugend 12th SS, he was putting himself to the final test.

His friends in the unit knew that he was having doubts as to whether he could command troops in battle. Every day he saw first-hand the high rate of battle casualties, including former students he had known at high school.

During a quiet chat, the CO offered **HUGHES** the opportunity to go to a Battle Exhaustion Centre. He quickly rejected this.

As an alternative, he was told that he could ask for a few days of LOB (Left Out of Battle). He would spend some time with an unofficial group which was made up of Black Devils who had had their share of combat. Such men were against being sent home and having to live with the knowledge that they were unable to meet the standards necessary for combat. This information could easily follow them into civil life after demobilization.

HUGHES chose to 'bunk in' at this special unit, established at the rear echelon of the battalion. He would find good fellowship and an opportunity to discuss his doubts about his ability to command troops.

A few days in these surroundings were sufficient to convince him that he could indeed withstand the rigours of combat and, at his own request, he was sent back to an infantry platoon.

Friends attested that he had left 'the tent,' full of desire to get back to his unit. The story has a sad ending, and his marble headstone can be found in Beny-sur-Mer Cemetery. It shows he was killed in action on August 12 '44 at the age of 28.

Hughes Island in Jordan Lake, Manitoba was named after him as part of the Manitoba Government's highly praised initiative to ensure that Manitobans killed in action would be remembered, not only by headstones in far-off countries, but as the names of lakes, islands and other geographical features which would carry their names through history.

Chapter 25

HEROES

I heard a voice that cried, "Make way for those that died!"
They Are All Heroes …

Sir John Squire's in "The March"

The statement about heroes is attributed to **Sir Douglas Bader** who served with the RAF as a fighter pilot. He had lost both legs in a flight training accident before World War II. Some were aghast when it was learned that, despite his handicap, he was engaged as a fighter pilot when WWII started, rising to the rank of Group Captain. **Sir Douglas** came to Ottawa at the invitation of The War Amps and fulfilled a number of speaking engagements. During a question-and-answer session in Ottawa, he was asked a question by the late Marjorie Nichols, who was one of our leading media experts. The question: "Sir Douglas, how do you define a hero?"

Sir Douglas had obviously been asked the question before. He looked at Marjorie and then at the crowd. His powerful voice rang out:

> "Lady, go visit the cemeteries. See their last resting places. Copy down the names and you will have a roster. They are all heroes."

This from a man who headed one of the fighter wings of the RAF. He was shot down and was lionized by none other than Herman Goering, the Chief of the German Air Force – himself a highly decorated fighter pilot from the First World War. At Goering's demand, the British sent a special plane to drop **Sir Douglas**' spare legs into the POW camp. It is known that **Sir Douglas** was the leader in organizing escapes. He was incarcerated in the infamous Colditz Castle – a fortress which Hitler and his generals stated to be 'escape-proof.' **Sir Douglas** failed in his later attempts to escape from Colditz!

Chapter 26

THE BACKBONE OF AN INFANTRY REGIMENT:

THE NCOs

*When the going gets tough,
the tough get going.*

Conn Smythe
Toronto Maple Leafs

The argumentative question is often heard - which is the best infantry regiment in the Canadian army? Comparisons are odious – and impossible. Moreover, none is required. It is a safe bet that the infantry regiments which included the RWRs could hold their own against the best that have been produced over centuries.

The surprising element is that the regiments of the 3rd Canadian Division were all recruited after the 1st and 2nd Divisions. In retrospect, this meant that the men were not the type who rushed in when war was declared. Also, they could not be classified as those who filled the gap of the ranks of the infantry after the 1st Division was mobilized. That was left largely for the 2nd Division. This meant that the 3rd Division encompassed men in their infantry ranks who joined up approximately ten months after World War II broke out. As a cross section of young Canadians, they were employed and some were settled into family life. The wonderment of it all is that from these divisions came a cadre of the finest NCOs that Canada has ever seen.

Many were in the RWR. Unfortunately, it is not possible to name them all in this memoir. A selection of some with whom I either trained or fought should provide a rough sketch of how these NCOs developed from citizens, not just to be soldiers – but the stalwart men who stood between the private soldier (riflemen if you wish) and the officers described elsewhere in this memoir.

At random then is a selection:

LANCE CPL AUSTIN FULLER from Rapid City, Manitoba, was respected by all. A rough, tough, but nice guy. He was 26 when the murderous 12th SS turned their machine guns onto **AUSTIN** and some 60 or so RWR. All had surrendered in noble fashion, had been searched and de-weaponed. They thought they were on their way to prison camp – which should have been their fate if the Geneva Conventions had been applied.

AUSTIN FULLER was the kind of NCO to whom an officer could give an order and know it would be carried out. Why? Firstly because he was that kind of soldier; secondly because his men would follow him anywhere.

AUSTIN died on June 8 '44 and is commemorated at Beny-sur-Mer Canadian War Cemetery in Calvados, France. He was the son of Stanley and Dorothy Fuller of New Westminster, British Columbia. *Fuller Lake* (64 B/12), southwest of Opachuanau Lake was named after him in 1981.

CPL ROGER FIRMAN from Transcona, a suburb of Winnipeg. His regimental number, H 40587, tells a story in itself. This means that he was the 87th recruit to come through the door of the Robinson Barracks in Winnipeg in 1940. It was anyone's guess as to his age in that he was only 21 when he was killed in cold blood while a Prisoner of War on June 8 '44. He is commemorated at Beny-sur-Mer Canadian War Cemetery in France. The author of this memoir remembers making out his Attestation papers on joining. He looked young then and he still looked young when his life was brutally taken from him in the largest mass murder of prisoners in the history of the modern British army; that is, when the 12th SS, on orders from **GERMAN GENERAL WILHELM MOHNKE,** executed the prisoners.

Those who escaped told the War Crimes Commission that the Germans behind the guns were battle hardened NCOs, some with experience on the Russian Front. **ROGER** is buried in the Beny-sur-Mer Canadian War Cemetery which is about 10 miles from Juno Beach. He was the son of Frederick and Emilie Firman of Transcona and was married to Vera. He is commemorated by the naming of *Firman Lake* (64 K/9), northeast of Lake Brochet.

CSM ALEXANDER GIBBS. It would be a safe bet to say that **ALEX GIBBS** was among the top ten NCOs of the Regiment. He was known in the ranks of the RWR as a good soldier, a great guy and a wonderful fellow to have as a friend. He enlisted in July '40, having come into Winnipeg on a draft from his hometown of Dauphin, Manitoba. He lasted nine months in action, which in itself must be some sort of record. He was killed on March 30 '45 and is buried at Groesbeek Canadian War Cemetery in Holland. His legion of friends would have been pleased indeed to know that *Gibbs Island* (63 P/11) in Partridge Crop Lake carries the name of **ALEX GIBBS**. It is a fond hope that anyone who visits this island will have an opportunity of learning a bit more about the wonderful soldier whose name the island now bears.

CPL HUGH MACKERRACHER was one of those members of the RWR whose name was known throughout the Regiment. He was decorated by what is known as MENTIONED IN DISPATCHES. For the non-initiated, this stands one level below the Military Medal. A MENTIONED IN DISPATCHES usually means that the man was recommended for a Military Medal or an even higher Gallantry Award but the powers-that-be might well have been overloaded with requests for gallantry medals and considered that the best they could do was to award **MACKERRACHER** with the 'MENTIONED.' He died on July 5 '44 and is commemorated at Beny-sur-Mer Canadian War Cemetery in Calvados, France. His geographic feature carrying the name of *MacKerracher Lake* (64 G/6) is east of Big Sand Lake.

Those of us who knew **HUGH** would be quick to say that he deserved the very highest in gallantry decorations; also it can only be hoped that future generations, seeing the name *MacKerracher Lake*, could know something of the fortitude of this man; could know something of the way the men under him adored him and the high respect in which he was held by his officers. (I can still see him in a grain field, charging a German Pill Box and yelling encouragement to his men.)

CPL RON MINAKER. Mention the name **RON MINAKER** to any RWR who soldiered with him right up until the day he was killed on the July 4 '44 and the picture of the perfect non-commissioned officer comes out.

His eagerness to serve his country was apparent. At the age of 17 he attempted to join the Fort Garry Horse – another Winnipeg Regiment which covered itself with glory when it landed on D-Day in support of the Eastern flank at Juno Beach. **RONNIE** joined the military District 10 Band and when he was old enough he transferred to the RWR. Many of the men of the Signal Platoon remembered him as he had graduated from the Royal Canadian Army Signal School in Barrie, Ontario. He was raised in Morris,

Manitoba and came from a military family. His father and uncle both served in WWI and his older brother saw service in WWII.

RONNIE is buried at Beny-sur-Mer Canadian War Cemetery in France. He was the son of George and Sarah Minaker of Winnipeg and was survived by his wife Agnes 'Gene' Minaker of St-Vital, a suburb of Winnipeg. He also had a daughter.

RON MINAKER is commemorated by the naming of *Minaker Creek* (54 B/10) in the Kaskattma River area.

Interlude

> Most infantrymen will tell you that the 'workhorse' of a platoon is the sergeant. He must establish keen rapport with his corporals, who are the commanders of the three sections. He is responsible for explaining the orders of the platoon commander, who is usually a lieutenant. The platoon sergeant, however, has the difficult task of being the disciplinarian, where the platoon commander, who is an officer, automatically has a bit of 'noblesse oblige.' The best explanation of why the men should follow an officer, no matter what, was when a platoon Sergeant turned and said: "After all, the officer has the radio link and the map. He is the only guy who can really get the platoon out of trouble, so listen up!"

We were blessed in the RWR with some tremendous NCOs. Set out below are a few 'thumbnail sketches' of other NCOs with whom I had personal contact and a close association ... but first a personal anecdote.

Near Bretteville-le-Rabet

The battalion 2 I/C's carrier came poking down the road. At the controls was **RFN KEN WOODCOCK** (later killed on March 30 '45 and commemorated by the naming of *Woodcock Lake* (64 F/2), northwest of Barrington Lake). **MAJ RUPE FULTZ**, the battalion 2 I/C at the time, always said that Woodcock was 'one hell of a soldier but couldn't drive a Model T Ford.' (Come to think of it, neither could most of us, with Henry Ford's 3-pedal gearshift mechanism – but that is another story.)

Ken lost control. The carrier slid and then flipped on its side leaving its passengers dazed. From out of a wheatfield came a tough-looking Wehrmacht NCO. He had won the coveted Iron Cross in Russia. Fear, however, exuded from his persona. He turned out to be a deserter, holding a Safe Conduct Pass.

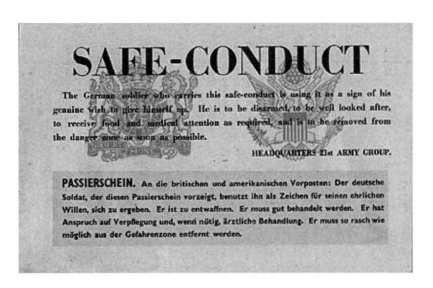

The RWRs were lying in a ditch while the upturned tracks of **Ken's** carrier spun gravel in all directions. The German NCO – a Feldwebel, the equivalent of our CSM – showed his Safe Conduct Pass. He had thrown his Schmeisser away. He was careful to give out some real friendly looks – unmistakably friendly. We were under observation fire from a German gun position. The Feldwebel had no inclination to turn away. In surrendering he was sending a message to others who might follow suit.

It was a sunny day and he was glad to share Canadian smokes, all of which led to some interesting conversation. He was giving **Cpl Everet (Ed) Werry** the once-over. His interest seemed genuine. This led to a question. He said something about 'where did these dynamic NCOs come from?' Fortunately, he knew enough English to carry on a conversation. A good friend of **Ed Werry's** filled in the blanks. It appeared that **Cpl Werry** had come from Crystal City, Manitoba.

Later it was possible to fill in a bit more of the history. On a recce near Big Sand Lake in Northern Manitoba after the war, we learned the following:

A commemorative certificate was presented to Ed's cousin and former RWRs commanding officer LIEUTENANT COLONEL RON E. WERRY. The honours were carried out by the HONOURABLE GIL MOLGAT, Hon. Col. Of the Regiment and Speaker of the Canadian Senate. The event was the annual dinner of the Royal Winnipeg Rifles commemorating the Battle of Fish Creek (1885).

Some of the RWRs lying in the ditches told the German deserter a few 'tid bits' of CPL WERRY'S acts of courage. WERRY explained the battle honours on his cap badge. The German NCO's ears pricked up when he heard the details of the Battle of Fish Creek – and of the date, 1885.

The German was a fan of United States westerns, and wanted to know if Wild Bill Hickok, Doc Holiday, etc., took part in the battle at Fish Creek. He was quickly apprised of a short history of the Northwest Rebellion. His admiration for NCOs whose forebears went back to 1885 seemed to rise even greater.

This German NCO wanted to know much more about Canadian NCOs and, from my diary, I was able to slake his thirst for knowledge.

CPL EVERET WERRY was later killed. The date was October 15 '44. He was 24 years old. He is commemorated at the Adegem Canadian War Cemetery in Belguin. He was the son of Luther and Margaret J. Werry of Winnipeg. *Werry Lake* (64 J/5), north of Big Sand Lake, was named after him in 1972.

It is instructive to look at the history of other gritty NCOs who 'put the boots' to the Germans, including the vaunted Hitler Youth. For example, there was SGT BOB ADAM, one of the early recruits who was somewhat older than the average rifleman (age 37) when he was killed on April 14 '45. Unfortunately, this was close to the end of the war. He is commemorated by the naming of *Adam Creek* (64 P/10) which flows southeast into Caribou River in Manitoba.

CPL JOSEPH PRAYZNER was killed on October 9 '44 in the Battle for the Leopold Canal. A mild-mannered soldier, but a 'take over' guy when the going got rough. He was the son of John and Helen Prayzner and was married. He often spoke about his wife, Ann, of Winnipeg. They also had one son. **JOE** was well known in Shoal Lake, Manitoba. He was active in hockey and was one of the few RWR who could claim having won archery titles.

He earned his Corporal stripes soon after joining the Regiment. Barrack-room talk was often about **PRAYZNER**. He was very popular and a great guy. Needless to say, he was a great soldier and sadly missed when he was killed.

He is buried in the Adegem Canadian War Cemetery in Belgium. He is commemorated in the geographical scheme of things by the Manitoba Government in *Prayzner Lake* (52 L/13) which is just south of Manigotagan Lake. Incidentally this brings an extra thump or two to my heart because as a kid I explored all the area around Lake du Bonnet which included the Manigotagan Lake.

SGT JAMES REID was from one of several Reid families who served in the RWRs. It is believed, from my discussions with him, that the others may have been cousins. At least two of them were invalided home before they saw action due to ill health. **JIMMY REID** was killed in the mass murder by the German SS on June 8 '44. He was 26 years of age and is buried at the Beny-sur-Mer Canadian War Cemetery just south of Juno Beach in France.

His brother, who also served in the RWRs, wrote a moving tribute to **JIM**. He told of a wonderful brother, skilled in a number of sports. He also mentioned that his brother played the guitar and was proficient in both skating and baseball. **JIM REID** is commemorated by the naming of *Reid Point* (63 N/8) in the File River. It is my privilege to say that I never served with a finer soldier.

SGT FRANK J. RYAN – Here was a Sergeant whose courage was beyond belief. He won the Military Medal – a very rare gallantry award. He was killed on July 6 '45 when he was 31 years of age.

He was survived by his wife, Sarah. His citation reads: "This soldier gave exemplary service." He was an outstanding non-commissioned officer and, as he was 31 and a little older than most other ranks, he did a remarkable job in providing essential information to younger recruits who came up to the Regiment. *Ryan Lake* (64 J/10), west of Tadoule Lake, was named after him.

SGT ORVILLE D. (ODEE) SMITH came from Selkirk, Manitoba – a prominent town on the Red River about 20 miles northeast of Winnipeg. His buddies had a lot of fun with his nickname. He hated the name **ORVILLE** and insisted that he be called by his initials - thus, **ODEE**.

He fought like a tiger from D-Day right through to the Leopold Canal. It is recalled how he jumped out of the Kapok and Canvas Boat which somehow turned sideways in the 24-foot wide Canal. The water was well over his head but he managed to straighten out the flimsy craft so that he and some of his platoon could get ashore. **ODEE** actually laughed after climbing the mud bank on the German side. He scarcely believed it when we told him that he was at last in Holland. The Leopold Canal is the border between Belgium and Holland at this particular location.

ODEE was a character. A letter written by his brother gives this description: "His friends always called him '**ORVILLE**' without shortening his name. Underneath his character, steel could be sensed. This only got him more respect and deepened friendships."

He was killed on October 12 '44 when he was 23 and is buried in the Adegem Cemetery in Belgium. He is commemorated by the naming of *Odee Smith Lake* (53 L/4) southwest of Bolton Lake in Manitoba.

LANCE SGT CHARLES E. TOURAND of Ste. Rose du Lac (H 42064) died July 4 '44 at the age of 25 and is commemorated at Beny-sur-Mer Canadian War Cemetery in France. He was the son of John and Marie L. Tourand of Laurier. *Tourand Lake* (64 P/1), southwest of Caribou Lake was named after him in 1974. A tough soldier who took his share of Germans – either dead or as POWs.

SGT HAROLD WALMSLEY was born in Bowsman River. He was one of the original Rifles with a Service Number H 40765. Reams could be written about **HAROLD WALMSLEY**. Perhaps it would suffice to say that he was the all-around great soldier. He was made Sergeant largely because he had earned the respect of his platoon. He was killed on July 4 '44 at the Battle of Carpiquet. He was 27 years old   He is buried at Beny-sur-Mer Cemetery just south of Juno Beach. He is commemorated by the naming of *Walmsley Lake* (64 I/12) which is located about 100 miles east of Hudson Bay. It is an area well known to trappers and hunters. Friends have often commented that this would have suited **HAROLD**. He was not only a great soldier but a great outdoorsman. He was once recommended for a commission but turned it down.

Authors Note: We have attempted in this section to give what might be called an overview of the tough, sensitive, intelligent NCOs who rose above the rank of Rifleman. They were looked up to by their men who served beneath them and by their officers who would have made the recommendation for their promotion to NCO rank.

Chapter 27

CRITICISM OF CANADIAN SOLDIERS

Read On . . .
The Historians and Generals Go On Record,
But They Never Got Close To The Action.

Guardsman 'Phil' Fillmore (Montgomery's staff)

The Comparison: German vs. Canadian

A comparison of the German versus the Canadian citizen soldier will help to understand how good our guys were!

The historian, with his documents and published material, searches for a controversy which will attract attention. After all it is part of his or her life.

Some 27 books and published lectures were issued in conjunction with the 60th Commemoration of D-Day in Normandy in June of '44.

In Normandy, the major issue to which reference was made concerns the fighting qualities of the Canadian ground troops vs. the German Army. Moreover, most authors seem to emphasize the 'downside'... that is, the 'questionable' performance of the Canadians. Our men usually bear the brunt of why it took some 25 days to close the gap between Caen and Falaise. Admittedly the Canadians trapped thousands of Germans but at stupendous casualty rates.

Moreover, the authors seem to go to great pains to remind all and sundry that the German fighter was vastly superior to his Canadian counterpart.[*] In actual fact, there is no need to defend the fighting capabilities of the Canadian soldier! The histories are proof that the Canadian soldier was simply good enough at his job to close the Falaise Gap. This meant driving back the German Armies. Much of the writing on Normandy simply ignores

---

[*] No such criticism is made against the Polish Armoured Division, which played an important role

that, to do this, he had to beat the seasoned storm troopers (and the reluctant but dangerous foreign 'conscripts') produced by the German military system.

The established authors who are quick to criticize the Canadians usually go back to ONE SINGLE SOURCE. It is in material originally written by no less than the Canadian Army's WWII historian … **COL CHARLES P. STACEY**. His opinion was highly publicized and gained considerable weight because of his position!

Some examples: **GEN CHARLES FOULKES** (The Victory Campaign, p. 276):

"When we went into battle at Falaise and Caen, we found that when we bumped into the battle-experienced German troops, we were no match for them."

Several more quotes are relevant. In a chapter titled 'Soldiers,' the noted British author **THOMAS HASTINGS** fires a broadside at the entire Canadian Army when he writes of *"xxx the glory of German arms in Normandy."*

The Distinguished military historian **JOHN GOOCH** (co-editor of a series on military history) says:

"Combat performance in the British Army (including Canadians) in Northwest Europe … has been measured against that of the German army and found to be wanting in almost every respect."

Carlo D'Este's *Decision in Normandy* is quoted in a recent book by **TERRY COPP**, military historian at Sir Wilfrid Laurier University, where he describes:

"the image of hesitant, un-aggressive Allied soldiers confronting bold, resolute Panzer grenadiers."

D'Este generalized from his questionable 'evidence' to argue that: *"the Anglo-Canadian armies lacked both leadership and combat effectiveness."*

None of these authors interviewed the fighting man, in person, relying almost wholly on Stacey's 'immortal' quote.

"It is not difficult to put one's finger upon occasions in the Normandy campaign when Canadian formations failed to make the most of their opportunities. In particular, the capture of Falaise was long delayed, and it was necessary to mount not one but two set-piece operations for the purpose at a time when an early closing of the Falaise Gap would have inflicted most grievous harm upon the enemy and might even, conceivably, have enabled us to end the war some months sooner than was actually the case. A German force far smaller than our own, taking advantage of strong ground and prepared positions, was able to slow our advance to the point where considerable German forces made their escape. That this was also due in part to errors of judgement south of the Gap should not blind us to our own shortcomings.

Had our troops been more experienced, the Germans would hardly have been able to escape a worse disaster."

Moreover, few of the authors knew, on a personal basis, the soldiers about whom they were writing. It seems essential that, if there is to be an understanding about the effectiveness of the German soldier compared with the citizen soldiers of the Canadians in Normandy, first hand knowledge of the latter is necessary.

This can be obtained in a number of ways. Firstly, the observer must have prior knowledge of the environment, family life, civil employment and other factors involving the Canadian soldier.

In an examination of the comparison, the objective of 'getting inside the soldier's head' is of prime importance. Thus, a reliable source is needed.

As indicated herein, many of the 'armchair' experts who write about Normandy are quick to find fault with our ground forces. If, as they state, the Canadian troops were lacking in leadership, training, and even courage, it should be examined as to who these men were.

What of their 'makeup?' Did they have enough 'gravel in the guts' to battle the skilled and ferocious German soldier at close quarters – and beat him at his job?

The task now lies before us. An explanation must be given in simple language in respect of what made the Canadian infantrymen 'tick.' The

German soldier was fighting for his life, including his escape to the Rhine and his own country. The Canadians, mostly volunteers, had a more simple reason to risk life and limb. They knew right from wrong! It proved to be a powerful stimulant.

No other inducements were necessary. Some ill-informed bystanders have said it was for glory. These people are not even worth a listen. Some have said it was for adventure. That idea disappeared from view when the first German attacks hit, whether it was in the air, on the sea, in the staging areas in England or in the areas where bitter fighting took place on land. Some said Canadian soldiers enlisted because they were unemployed and they needed a job. Check the records on enlistment. Most were labourers, farm help or other seasonal workers. Does anyone believe they would give up whatever money they could earn on 'Civvy Street' for $1.30 a day – and a lottery ticket to a grave in some far off land?

Chapter 28

THE PRIVATE SOLDIER OF THE ROYAL WINNIPEG RIFLES

Show me the two so closely bound
As we, by the wet bond of blood,
By friendship, blossoming from mud,
By Death: we faced him, and we found
Beauty in Death.

Robert Graves, Poet of England
Beauty in Death

The Private Soldier

Soldiers without rank in a Rifle Battalion are never called privates. They are 'Riflemen.' Also, the usual commands of ATTENTION, STAND AT EASE and STAND EASY are never heard. It is traditional in Rifle Battalions to replace the command ATTENTION by simply repeating the name of the formation. For example, if a sergeant major wanted to call his troops to attention, he would use the command 'Stand To Your Front, Company' or 'Stand To Your Front, 17 Platoon.'

In this regard, reference is made to the need herein for a description of the private soldier (Rifleman).

Their job was made somewhat easier because, taking for example the RWR. It developed into a homogenous group that made up the fighting men known as The Little Black Devils.

A mosaic of the ordinary soldier would see a smattering of:

- Rural boys who made their living before the war working on harvesting gangs, as road builders, etc.
- Boys from the outskirts and the inner cities.
- Metis/Treaty Indians/Inuit.

In training the boys from the rural or suburban areas would be lying side by side with a runner from a Winnipeg Cold Storage Plant or an apprentice mechanic who had worked on automobiles. What the rural boy didn't know, he could pick up from the lads from the inner cities – and there would be 'cross pollination.'

The rural boys picked up, by osmosis, enough inner city smarts to get by. On the other hand, the boys from the cities would learn their field craft the hard way, scrabbling through the prairie fields, amply dotted with stones from the days that the land was cleared, or the ever-present mud holes.

The average age of a rifleman would run somewhere between 18 and 35. Their physical condition was excellent, simply because most had lived hard lives. Also, by constant association, there was a silent 'getting to know you.'

These are the same boys whose dead bodies were seen scattered through the waist-high grain fields after a battle.

Today they are gathered under headstones in two major Canadian cemeteries, Beny-sur-Mer and Bretteville-sur-Laize. Here is a selection.

RFN ERNIE BASKERVILLE of Mayfield, Manitoba died on June 8 ' 44. He was 21 years of age. He was one of nearly 60 RWRs who had been taken prisoner, disarmed and marched into a German-held field. It was my privilege to give evidence at the war crimes trials. The information which went to the court, under the chairmanship of **BRIG HARRY FOSTER**, is bloodcurdling.

ERNIE looked about 15. He was an excellent soldier. In speaking with some who escaped, I have often wondered what went through the minds of **ERNIE BASKERVILLE** and the others when they realized that the Germans, with their machine guns mounted on half-tracks or trucks, had opened fire. Certainly in **ERNIE'S** background there was nothing to prepare him for this shock.

We can assume that **ERNIE BASKERVILLE'S** first thought, when he saw the Germans getting ready to shoot into the group of RWRs, was disbelief. Gratefully, this would have lasted only a few minutes, as the Germans were not about to waste ammunition. Most of the group (five escaped) were mown down by rapid fire machine gun bullets.

ERNIE'S was not what might be expected as the normal death of a soldier. He was not killed during an attack up a hill ... he was not hit by a shell, random or otherwise. Instead, he must have faced the awful truth that he was to be killed the minute the German machine gunners opened up.

According to the evidence at the trial, none of the soldiers flinched. Some shook hands. Some cried 'Mother.' Some were heard uttering the names of their wives. Some vowed that their love of family would stand the test of time.

The shooting of prisoners in cold blood was not an everyday occurrence. It happened mostly with the 12 SS Hitler Jugend (average age: 18) – soldiers who swore allegiance to ADOLF HITLER and killed with wild abandon and, quite obviously, some elation.

ERNIE was with the Rifles only a short time, as he had transferred from a Saskatchewan unit. Those RWR soldiers who survived, however, were quoted in a letter in regard to his commemoration with the naming of *Baskerville Lake* (64 P/10), east of Nejanilini Lake. The naming was carried out in 1974.

His brother recalls:

> "Ernie, as he was affectionately called, was born in Hazlet, Saskatchewan. Because of the dustbowl of the Dirty Thirties, the family moved to Mayfield, Manitoba. Ernie loved farming… the work was hard, especially during seeding and harvesting. He always found time to repair the family automobile. He had a trapline in winter to earn a few extra dollars. Hunting deer in the fall was not just a sport, but a necessity. Ernie was an excellent shot. He was a happy person with a contagious smile."

RFN FRED BLAIR died an unusual death on August 23 '43. The Regiment had been sent to Inverary, Scotland for assault training. His widow, Margaret Blair of Rochdale, Lancashire, England, said:

"I am not aware of the exact area in England or Scotland my husband was in when he was killed; all I know is that they were using live ammunition on a manoeuvre, resulting in his death. He is buried in my hometown of Rochdale. I was receiving a War Widows Pension until I remarried."

Note: The marriage was in 1942. The Government of Canada reinstated all pensions to war widows, regardless of whether they were remarried. This was on June 29 '89. The Service Bureau of The War Amputations of Canada wrote to Mrs. Blair several weeks after being notified that she was eligible to have her pension on behalf of **FRED** reinstated irrespective of whether she remarried.

Blair Island (63 K/16) in Loonhead Lake was named after him in 1973.

LANCE CPL RON BROOKS was born in Pilot Mound, Manitoba and died on February 16 '45 at the age of 22. This means, as will be obvious, that he saw a lot of action as a very young man.

After **RON** was killed his brother received a letter from a friend telling the details of **RON'S** death. It is appropriate to include some quotes:

"On the day Ron was killed, our platoon had its orders to go and take out a group of farm buildings; but our section was the only one to get action, and we took the house out and 86 prisoners and we sure dug into it. About 15 minutes later, they (the Germans) started to mortar fire and a mortar landed on the edge of Ron's trench.

He never knew what hit him, he died instantly. But he had a flesh wound in the leg before and I bandaged it and ordered him to go back, but he wouldn't go as there was only four of us left out of ten. Ron wasn't cut or bruised by the mortar and I will say he had guts and I shall never forget him. Together we had some of the best sections in the Company and now I am again with only three men and myself left. We buried Ron in Germany; but he was to be lifted and taken back to Holland and I think by this time he has been."

RON BROOKS is buried in Groesbeek Canadian War Cemetery in Holland. This was on the orders of the Canadian High Command who said that in so far as possible, any Canadians killed in Germany would be moved to the permanent Canadian War Cemetery in Groesbeek. It is possible to stand at the south-eastern edge of the Cemetery and overlook miles and miles of Germany. *Brooks Rapids* (64 P/15) in the Caribou River was named after him.

Chapter 29

FRIENDLY FIRE AND BODY BAGS (NORMANDY VERSION)

Experience teaches slowly and at the cost of mistakes

James A. Froude

It was a bright afternoon. The RWR had been ordered to dig in at a defensive position just north of Soulangy. Life looked pretty good, particularly when the Quartermaster dropped off a couple of two-quart jugs of rum.

Slowly a cry came from our rear echelon. It mentioned that the Yank Flying Fortresses were going to soften up Jerry before we had to attack at night.

Suddenly the roars of approval from the troops changed tone. Cries of terror came from behind a hill to the north of us.

It was almost too much to believe. We were being rained upon by sticks of explosives from the American bombers which were probably six or seven miles in the air.

MAJ HUGH DENISON was our Air Liaison Officer (ALO). We heard him on the battalion radio net warning the Regiment to take cover – we were being attacked from the skies. The bombs were coming from American Flying Fortresses, which we had learned to identify in our aircraft recognition seminars. Soon the ground was erupting all around us. **RFN HAROLD PROUT** stood up calling my name and asking what was to be done. I tried to sound encouraging. I said we would obviously be in radio contact and call off the attack. The information proved to be false.

A Regina Rifle was on his feet running around the slit trenches. The poor bugger was on fire. Some of the guys set out to catch him and perhaps roll a gas cape over him, but he was moving too fast. He was burned alive.

By this time, many of the original RWR who had landed on D-Day could call themselves seasoned soldiers. **SGT DON MCGEACHIE** – an extremely brave NCO – stood up and repeated the order: 'Take cover!'

In an attempt to ward off the marauding aircraft, we fired smoke bombs. The aircraft was much higher than our range. One of our better soldiers was **EVERHARD DAVIS**. He had shown that he had ample guts. On D plus 5 he had gone out and retrieved at least five German Schmeisser MGs and brought back some POWs with him.

Every man has his storehouse of courage. When it runs out, little can be done. I had bunked in with **EVERHARD DAVIS** as far back as Shilo. Hence, I was watching him carefully. He was running around the bombed out area doing whatever he could.

He would cut away battledress, find bandages which were usually stored in the netting of the tin hat and pour sulpha into open wounds. His actions were beyond heroic. In view of his actions when he was a raw recruit, I was a bit concerned but as I looked closely at his face, he was 'calm, cool and collected,' as they say.

As he got up and left his slit trench, I tried to stop him. As it turned out, **EVERHARD** rolled over on top of me. He was a rather big man and I am not ashamed to say that I felt a little safer from the friendly fire.

We settled down when I reminded him that he was the only batman who had served two corporals. The story was classic. The major commanding the company had wanted to dismiss him under Section 15 as 'unlikely to become an efficient soldier.' My God, was he wrong!

EVERHARD, looking like a peeping gopher that he had often seen perched on his hind legs in the grain fields north of Brandon, took one look and yelled that something had to be done. At least six RWRs were lying only yards away. Some were suffering with their tender guts hanging out. Others had lost limbs or had sustained horrible head wounds.

Hard to believe, but here was **EVERHARD DAVIS** – 'unlikely to become an efficient soldier' – moving among all the wounded, telling them 'you're OK,' and doing what he could to make them comfortable as he gathered shell dressings, sulfa and morphine. He eased the suffering of at least four of his buddies with whom he had soldiered all the way from Winnipeg, Manitoba. How he managed to stay alive with the American bombs bouncing all over at least three acres of ground, no one will ever know.

His last act in the devastation of the bombing was sheer compassion. I saw him lay his lanky frame on top of **SGT WILLIAM CALMAIN**. He was attempting to bring peace and quietness in what was obviously the last few minutes that **BILL** would know of life as a soldier.

This kind of bravery was commonplace among the seasoned troops of our gallant Western battalion.

EVERHARD survived the war, got home to his wonderful wife Cathy, fathered two beautiful girls, and lived to conquer a serious belly wound while at the same time driving a truck from Winnipeg to Toronto and back. Do they make those kinds of guys any longer? Hopefully it will not take another major conflict on the battlefields in Europe to find the answer.

SGT WILLIAM CALMAIN was 25 years of age when he died August 16 '44. He is buried at Bretteville-sur-Laize Canadian War Cemetery in France. He was the son of William and Ida Calmain of Winnipeg. *Calmain Lake* (63 J/13) north of Wekusko Lake was named after him.

Body bags were not in use in World War II. In order to avoid bloating or spread of disease with blowflies, the bodies of those who were killed would be covered with gas capes, blankets or, in a necessity, grass, twigs or sod.

The term 'friendly fire' was not in use either. If a Canadian soldier was hit, it was more than likely that the artillery round carried a faulty fuse. Another likelihood would be mortars, which were not terribly accurate. The system for aiming the smaller 25-pounder artillery or the mortar was to seek out a target with a ranging gun from the dug in battery of the 25 pounders or from the usually closer mortars of the battalion, or the 4.2 mortars of the Cameron Highlanders of Ottawa.

The procedure to find a correct target was simplicity in itself. For example, from the 25 pounder ranging gun, the call was for one round ranging. If it was off the mark, another round was fired, bringing it either up or down in elevation or right / left for traversing. When the ranging gun was dead on target, the company commander, could order a full shoot.

The secret was that at the ranging gun (or mortar as the case may be) when the shell was dead on target, the person in charge would hammer a metal stake in the ground with a round white aiming point. This would give the other guns or mortars the exact position and the shoot could progress.

I am no expert but all officers did take part in ranging and operating both mortars and 25 pounders in training.

Although this is a rudimentary explanation, it might give some idea as to how whole batteries (and more) of 25 pounders and medium and heavier artillery guns and mortars could be effective. During Normandy, the personnel using these weapons were highly skilled; thus, they were very effective both in attack and defence.

Chapter 30

THE INNS OF COURT REGIMENT

'We are still masters of our fate. We are still captain of our souls.'

Sir Winston Churchill

In August '44 a call came from the RWR adjutant's office. My name had been requested as a witness for a Court of Enquiry. The charge was that the Inns of Court Regiment had used German prisoners as 'human shields.' Presumably some of the facts were known to me. I was sent to the headquarters of the British Div, where I was sworn in to give evidence.

The officer in charge of F Troop of the Inns of Court was **Lt Doug Sewell**. His task, following the landing on the Normandy beaches, was to keep track of movements for the Green Howards – one of the British regiments to which he was attached. He was detailed to carry out scouting missions in enemy-held territory.

I had first met him at battle school at Durham Castle in England. He had been fighting **Rommel's** troops in the desert near El Alamein. He knew his trade and was absolutely without fear. His men respected him.

I was with **Lt Sewell** when some of his scout cars of the Inns of Court returned from a recce in territory held by the enemy. Some German officers were sprawled on the front of **Sewell's** scout cars. They came to the position held by **Lt Sewell**. I was an eye witness, as my carriers were occupying the same vantage point. The German officers were antagonistic and were screaming that they had been in great danger, sitting on the front of the Inns of Court scout cars. 'Human shields' was not a term we used in World War II but, in describing their situation, they suggested that it was against the rules of war to carry prisoners in exposed positions.

It was months later that the British held a Court of Enquiry. The officers defending **Sewell** were working in a tent which looked like the officers' mess. We went over the details. I was warned by them to be absolutely neutral in giving my evidence. Obviously, **Sewell** was on trial for what the British, whether they won the war or not, considered was a criminal offence under the Geneva Conventions – placing the German officers in harm's way, without good reason.

There was no time for me to dress up for the occasion. Moreover, I had no intention of doing so. I appeared at the church basement where the trial was being held. The representatives of the British Army, including several Provost Marshals and the Judge Advocate General's (JAG) legal staff, were waiting. They had on their best serge uniforms, complete with Sam Browne belts, polished buttons, etc.

When I was ushered in, I could hear a gasp from the three-man board. I refused to take off my battle smock and helmet. My boots still carried the crud of the Normandy battleground. My face was grimy, except where my goggles had protected my eyes. In honour of the occasion, I had managed only a rough shave, using hot water heated in my mess tin over the motor of our carrier.

With proper British protocol, the terms of reference for the Board of Inquiry were read in stentorian tones by a puffed-up British half-colonel. He then asked me to report on the circumstances as I saw them.
It was difficult for me to remain impartial. I stated that, in my opinion, the German officers were in much greater danger if let loose even in their own lines. The safest place for them would be in the Allied POW 'cage.'

There was another factor in my mind: the officers, part of the SS Panzer Grenadiers, would shoot their own men for desertion if they found that any of them were 'on the loose.' It was my firm opinion that, from a tactical point of view, the Inns of Court were in fact protecting the lives of the German officers by making sure that they reached our Prisoner of War compound.

These staff wallahs, who had probably not seen a shot fired in anger, were somewhat perturbed that a rough-talking Canadian officer refused to kowtow to their haughty appearance. The legal officer conducting the board then asked me what I knew about the situation.

A stenographer or a tape recorder would have captured my sarcasm. One look at the stiff-necked British board made it clear they were trying to crucify **LT SEWELL** – a guy who had fought in the desert and who had made his weight felt in Normandy as well.

My description of the circumstances commenced with a question by me. The three-man board looked shocked when I asked whether they had any idea of the fluidity of the battle being waged during our invasion of Normandy. The Chairman of the Board (a full-colonel) gave me a withering look but answered negatively. This set the stage. I told them what the battlefield was like … dead, wounded, Germans hiding. In all, a dangerous environment. At one point my question was whether they knew what a Moaning Minnie was? Blank stares from them.

Getting to the meat of my evidence, I again asked a question of the board. It was along the lines of how they would bring back important German prisoners on scout cars which carried a small crew in a tight fit. My evidence was that if **LT SEWELL** was to leave these prisoners behind, they would be shooting at our own men the next day.

There is no shame in realizing that I was putting on a bit of an act. In my view, the British officers conducting this inquiry deserved to be told the circumstances regarding the manner in which **LT SEWELL'S** troop had brought back some ardent Nazi officers. Just as I was getting warmed up, the JAG representative suggested an adjournment. We left the room. It took only minutes for the Board of Inquiry to report that they would exonerate **SEWELL**. I had done my job.

It was not realized until afterward that this was a big deal. The Germans had accused the Inns of Court of forcing German captives to ride on the outside of the scout cars. My report to our adjutant (copied from my daily dairy):

```
In my evidence, I told the Board that there was no
other way that the German prisoners could be brought
back.  Also it was explained to the Board that the
prisoners could not sit on the rear part of the scout
cars.  To do so would expose them to the exhaust grids.
The Inns of Court could not march the captured Germans.
They would have escaped on foot.  Case dismissed!
```

THE INNS OF COURT REGIMENT

The Inns of Court Regiment of the British Army derives its name from the requirement that officers must be lawyers. The legal system in England requires generally that persons wishing to become barristers or solicitors must belong to one of the famous Inns of Court. These are private clubs surrounding Old Bailey, which is more or less the Supreme Court for cases reaching the highest level in England. The name Inns of Court evokes immediate interest.

Chapter 31

DID THE TOUGH GUYS REALLY SHOOT THEIR OFFICERS?[*]

Soldiers only know the street
Where the mud is churned and splashed about
By battle-wending feet;
And yet beside on stricken house there is a glimpse of grass.
Look for it when you pass

Edward Wyndham Tennant

The tiny village of Aubigny played an important role in the closing of the Falaise Gap. Aubigny was prefaced by a much larger battle centred on the town of Soulangy.

MAJ LOCKIE FULTON, the CO of Dog Company, had been called to Battalion HQ. Command of the company was left to me as Coy 2 I/C. We had secured Soulangy. Jerry had hidden Panther tanks behind brick walls. The town included a smattering of barns, French farmhouses and a church.

About 9:00 p.m. on August 16th, the Battalion 2 I/C, **MAJ RUPE FULTZ,** sent for me to meet him in a large barn. It was most remarkable for the number of fleas which had made their homes in it. The only advantage I could see was that this was going to be a very short 'Orders Group.' None of us, including **MAJ FULTZ**, were on friendly terms with the little black insects. They got into the seams of your battledress. A partly-open shirt front was also an invitation for a visit. They could inflict a very hard bite, escape, and wait for the chance to do it all over again.

MAJ FULTZ said this patrol was to be a small show. The objective: To connect with the Canadian 2nd Infantry Division which was holding the ground immediately to our right. I went back to my slit trench and looked for a 'volunteer.'

---

[*] Apparently the practice was widespread in Vietnam and was called 'Fragging' - - so called because the weapon of choice was a fragment grenade.

None of the 'old timers' were around. A soldier by the name of **Sgt Bill Scorgie** from Toronto was having a nap. Just the kind of guy if we ran into trouble was my thought. We commandeered a jeep and headed south on a side-road toward Falaise. **Bill** had gotten himself on friendly terms with the fleas. They seemed adept at making the jump from him to my own good self. Not knowing **Scorgie** well, I remarked that there were *beaucoup de fleas* crawling around outside the neck of his battledress. His reply quickly gave me a clue to his character. He said that the little buggers had found their way in – let them find their way out! We hid the jeep as we were getting close to Aubigny and could be spotted by the Germans. **Bill** told me that his father had been gassed in World War I. The family moved from Manitoba to Toronto. This I learned as we crawled along a ditch looking for signs of the 2nd Div.

Our friends, the fleas, were still with us and I felt an urgent necessity either to lag behind **Bill** or get well in front of him.

He scarcely knew me, but felt that our acquaintanceship was such that he could have a little fun.

The story has an important element. When an officer and a private go together on a dicey 'mission,' a sign of weakness by the officer might give the soldier the idea that his leader, by reason of rank, could mean trouble … with the private soldier picking up the cheque.

The quirk in **Bill Scorgie's** nature became fairly obvious. We had not been in battle together before. There were two other strikes against me. **Scorgie** came from a really tough part of Toronto. My home was Winnipeg. People from the 'Peg and those from 'Hogtown' (Toronto) sometimes had difficulty in understanding each other's point of view.

Crawling along the ditch was slow going for me ahead of **Scorgie**. He seemed also to be holding back a bit. With a smirk on his face, he asked whether I was about to dump him. He let fly with some remarks such as 'maybe I had a case of yellow fever.' I did not reply. He continued to fire 'cheap shots' at me. I did not respond. That was a mistake. It opened the door for **Scorgie**. He felt he could take a few more 'shots.' I could hear him uttering words like 'cold feet.' Again I did not reply. Another mistake. He abandoned all pretence. He was pushing the envelope with insults and even some outright abuse. There was no one else within earshot. He caught up to me and asked whether my silence was a case of being 'windy,' i.e., fear! His torrent of ridicule continued.

He started using terms like 'buck fever.' He asked whether I was feeling a bit of the 'pucker.' This was Army slang for when the muscles of the rear end tightened in tense situations.

Gradually **SCORGIE** got the better of me. I signalled him to take the lead. He pretended not to understand. My action loosened his tongue even further. He was having fun making unflattering comments about me and about officers in general.

Daylight had deserted us, but the ground was bathed in moonlight. Some shadowy shapes were noticed in the ditches on the other side of the road. I asked where the hell they came from. If there was a password, I had certainly forgotten it.

Their reply: To throw several hand grenades over the road. 'Ye Gads!' They were Germans. The grenades landed fairly close. We needed a plan and in a hurry. The edges of a shadowy culvert were spotted ahead. This called for a dash, with **SCORGIE** close behind. The culvert was full of offal, but was passable. A stone's throw away, partly hidden, was what looked like a German outpost with three or four soldiers on guard. I motioned to **SCORGIE** and I heard him cock his Sten gun. The Germans were firing in our direction. I circled behind them and returned their fire. Then did a fast crawl to their position. Two were dead. Presumably the others had taken off.

We decided it would not hinder our patrol. From **SCORGIE**, I heard something like 'nice work.' But he was not going to leave it at that. He added: 'jerk.' There was some satisfaction, though, when he murmured, presumably to himself but loud enough for me to hear: "Knows a little about his job, anyways."

As I crawled from the culvert, the unmistakable odour of unburied bodies assailed my nostrils. It is a difficult smell to describe but once experienced, it occupies a space in the olfactory nerves. In the moonlight I could see bodies where enemies on both sides had used the dreaded bayonet to kill. Lectures taught us that the Germans hated 'cold steel.' It is not difficult to understand why. (Incidentally those soldiers who have seen front line service will realize that these short paragraphs tell a truth unknown to those who have not had to eat, dig or sleep in the vicinity of decaying soldiers.)

Bayonet attacks were very rare in the ground warfare of World War II. When the horrible smell reached **SCORGIE** his body reacted and he asked me about the odour. We could see some dead soldiers from both sides who had lain unburied for some days in the summer heat. A rifle, held firmly to the torso by a bayonet was visible. **SCORGIE** immediately affixed his own bayonet – part of his Lee Enfield rifle he obviously thought he would never have to use.

The Germans were on a standing patrol. **SCORGIE** then showed his real stuff. He asked me to stay put and he would follow them down an old paved track. He stopped to put extra socks over his boots. I was puzzled. He told me that hobnailed boots made a hell of a noise. He came back with four prisoners. One was holding a leaflet which said something about surrendering and they would be safe. We told them to take off back in the direction of our lines and to talk loudly. We spent the rest of the night in their position. I was surprised at how deep the enemy soldiers had dug. There was even a ledge where we could get some sleep.

We found out one other thing. The Germans had left behind some gooey ointment. Thoughts of a Brylcreem ad that we had seen all around England came to mind. 'A little dab'll do ya.' We pasted some of the German's concoction around our neck and hands. The fleas were gone. I had my 18-set with me, and contacted company headquarters. Some flattering comments but the next news wasn't quite so welcome. Our little patrol was to hold the position and send back any information when the 2nd Div caught up to us.

Squeezed rather tightly together in the Germans' idea of a small trench, **SCORGIE** dropped his antagonism and told me that I had gotten them out of a real screw-up. There was now a pleasant tone in his words. Maybe an officer, even from Winnipeg, could gain acceptance of a tough kid from the harsh district of Toronto.

The battle for Aubigny was far from over. The next day, the CO sent up the remnants of two platoons. We were badly under strength, due to the fallacy of the politicians in Ottawa who seemed to be more afraid of conscription than they were of letting their troops fight with less than 50 per cent of our strength as called for in the Battle Order.

The story might have ended there, except that I actually began to enjoy SCORGIE. He was a character. He used phrases like 'having the hots' for a certain girl in England. He called her a 'real seven-day gasser,' whatever that meant. He said she could perform little tricks which were out of this world. I really didn't want to hear about them! SCORGIE had a way with the English language though – a way which definitely sounded out of sync with us boys from the west. Notwithstanding, he showed no fear; he was one hell of a soldier and he proved it.

Four or five days later, the CO asked me to take a night patrol along a railway embankment. I was doing my best (socks over shoes – a trick I learned from a Toronto soldier). When darkness came, I heard a gruff voice behind me and could feel a muzzle in my back. We had run into a German outpost.

Was BILL SCORGIE fooling me all along? Did he really hate officers all that much? Then I heard him utter the sweetest words. In his Toronto twang, he told the German not to threaten his officer. He said *"son of a bitch"* in German. The muzzle at my back was held by a Jerry who had infiltrated our patrol. SCORGIE had disarmed the German.

He then did something which is hard to forget. He asked me for my pistol, emptied all the rounds, and threw it at the German, who caught it in his right hand. I was mystified. SCORGIE said that it was an old city boy's trick. If you wanted to find out if a guy giving you trouble was left- or right-handed, you threw an empty pistol at him. Automatically he would catch it with the hand he used most. The mystery thickened. He then said, although the German couldn't understand him, that he was going to take pity on him. He would let his own troops dispose of him – that is, the Germans. Then, very neatly, he shot off two of the fingers of the German's left hand, then pushed him back over the railway embankment to his own troops. I said, "What goes?"

SCORGIE said, "We don't want to take him back as a prisoner and we don't want to shoot him." This way the Germans would think it was an SIW (self-inflicted wound) and the German battle police would charge him. The result? In all likelihood, he would be patched up and sent to the Russian front in a German CONVICTS Regiment. If this was impossible, he would certainly spend a few years in the German equivalent of a 'crowbar hotel.'

All of this intrigued me. I then began to realize the life that **SCORGIE** had lived before he enlisted. He must have run with some very tough guys. The idea of finding out whether an enemy was right- or left-handed could be important. **SCORGIE** knew the way this was done in the underworld: disarm your enemy, then throw him a pistol. He will catch it with his good hand. From then on, you could deal with him in any way you liked.

BILL SCORGIE died on August 28 '44 which was 16 days after the episode at Aubigny. He was 28 years old. He is buried at the Bretteville-sur-Laize Cemetery and is commemorated by the naming of *Scorgie Lake* (53 L/5) which is north of Bolton Lake in Manitoba. I received a letter from a friend of his. I would like to quote from it here:

> *His father had been badly gassed during World War I and suffered much from that during the years that I knew the family. I believe the father died during World War I. During the war, the family moved to the Toronto area. I was away in the army at that time as I was a couple of years older than William. He joined the army and came to our regiment as a reinforcement when we were in the Caen area. I saw him twice around that time, and then I went out wounded on August 15 and returned to the regiment early in October. When I went to look him up I found out he had been wounded (I think) around Calais. He died from those wounds.*

Why include this story? Some 'wiseacre' has said that officers who were unpopular got shot in the back. To me, this is a damned lie! Not that all officers were great – but most soldiers realized a few salient facts about them:

1. The officers knew the plan – how to get in and how to get out.
2. The officers carried the maps.
3. The officers had the radio link.
4. The officers gave the orders.
5. Most officers who fought in Normandy were the envy of the German soldiers (many of them conscripts from other armies).

In short, shoot your officer and you are likely to get confused – a recipe for disaster in a fluid war zone.

To finish this story, I was being propelled in a wheelchair down Aldershot in England. Both legs were encased in plaster of Paris. I was also wearing what they called a 'spike,' which was a very uncomfortable covering of plaster of Paris to hold up the wounded right arm.

A number of younger army reinforcements, who obviously had not yet been in battle, lined up and saluted me. "What the hell was that all about," I asked. They said that they realized now the job that officers had to do in war.

The reason of putting in this chapter on 'shooting your officers' is that a lot of stories came out of places like Vietnam about how the other ranks would shoot their officers, and they had a name for it – they called it fragging. Well, I can tell you this. I was four months in continuous action in Normandy. Not only did I never see evidence of an officer being shot by his own troops, but I never even heard of it.

Chapter 32

SHAKESPEARE – MY KINGDOM FOR A HORSE

Deeds, not words shall speak me

John Fletcher

The Falaise Gap was closed and thousands of Germans were trapped. It was August 27 '44.

The Canadian Army and the 1st Polish Armoured Division carried much of the fighting in Normandy in the Eastern Section. The Allies had taken about 10,000 German prisoners. The mood of our guys could be described as 'slap-happy.' Charlie Company was walking along the north bank of the Dives River, heading for Trun. My lead platoon spied a white horse in a farmyard. With a little help from the boys, I managed to get up on it – bareback. It was quite a sight as we travelled the miles between towns like Fresne-la-Mer and Crocy and along the north bank of the Dives River.

We had become friendly with the First Polish Armoured Division, most of which was across a ditch from us. They said later they liked the way the Canadians fought.

A Polish officer approached. He was yelling, "Shakespeare – Shakespeare" and in Polish he was shouting "Moje Królestwo Za Konia" (My kingdom for a horse)! We had plenty of Polish boys in the Winnipeg Rifles and translation was no problem. What could not be understood was why this Polish officer let it be known that he wanted the white horse very badly. The reason was understandable when explained.

Germany attacked Poland in September of 1940. The Polish Army was largely composed of cavalry, with the officers mounted on horses.

To get to the story itself, the Polish officer was saying, in Polish: "By God, I started this war on a white horse! I want to finish it off the same way!" Having seen the Falaise Gap closed, the Pole was under the impression that the war was over. The only fitting closure for him would be to ride herd on the German prisoners, astride a white horse. His rank: very high – at least a Brigadier.

The RWRs were indebted to the Polish Army. Time and again, Polish troops had neutralized German gun and mortar batteries which were killing off Canadians.

One episode tells the story. Charlie Company of the RWRs, which was under my temporary command, was detailed to capture the ground north of the Dives River. Not easy. The Germans were evacuating the area in small bunches. They often put up stiff rear-guard battles in farmhouses. Our casualties from these engagements were both sad and numerous.

The Germans were occupying a large farm complex. On the outskirts, more than 30 members of the Chaudière Regiment were lying feet first toward the road. All of them were dead, waiting for a priest.

The Black Devils were told to liquidate the stubborn German defenders. It was night-time. My interpreter told a Polish officer in a tank, that if we could not move the Jerries, my platoon would be sitting ducks at daylight. The Germans would have a clear field of fire. The Polish major was asked to do something which tank commanders would rather not do – that is, take his tank out at night and accompany the infantry along the attack route.

Nonetheless, he gave up his safe position in an orchard. It was a welcome sound for us to hear the Polish tank start up. Through our interpreter and the telephone which was mounted on the rear of the tank, he made it clear that it was not part of the tactics of the Polish Armoured to move at night without a guide. We agreed and sent one of our best trackers – a Métis with a bed sheet pinned to his back – along the route to be taken by the Polish tank. It worked. The Germans, realizing that to retreat was the better part of valour, vacated their heavily-fortified farm.

Back to the Trun area and the bridge. Come daylight. There were no Germans to be seen around the bridge at the Dives River. On the far side, our Polish Brigadier was riding his white horse.

A signal came back to our battalion headquarters. We still needed the bridge. 'Okay. Make sure it is in our hands.'

At this point **SGT ART KELLY** was absolutely certain that his company commander (me) had lost his marbles. When I laid out the plan for the attack, it met with loud guffaws from **KELLY**. He said that it made absolutely no sense to attack a bridge which the Germans could easily have used as a defence. He said it was obvious from the Pole on the white horse that the Polish were in possession of the ground on the far side of the Dives River.

Our plan had been okayed by the CO. It called for artillery support with a start time. At precisely 0900 hours, Charlie Company approached the bridge area with a false air of nonchalance. Surely the Germans were not bothered by the one Polish officer on a white horse. No - they were waiting for the Winnipegs. We still had to take that bridge. As Jerry opened up with his mortars and MGs, a valuable lesson was learned.

One Pole mounted on a horse, did not necessarily mean that no Germans occupied the other side of the Dives. My war diary entry said the fire fight lasted at least an hour. The Germans were eventually routed. It was not a foolish gesture simply to rescue the Polish officer and the white horse. We did indeed capture the bridge, but it proved to be a difficult objective.

The story has a rather beautiful sequel. In February of 1999, the Polish military attaché in Ottawa, armed with the story of the white horse, approached the Canadian Prime Minister's office. A visit to Warsaw was being planned for the P.M. Our military intelligence tracked me down. As a result I accompanied **PRIME MINISTER JEAN CHRÉTIEN** to Poland.

The occasion of the PM's visit, at least in part, was to commemorate a remarkable monument which was eventually placed in front of the Canadian Embassy in Warsaw. The shrine is outstanding. The Polish people had found a large oblong-shaped stone measuring ten feet long and five feet high. The next step was to locate a similar-sized stone in Canada. The Polish community in the Ottawa Valley took up the challenge. A similar-sized stone was found near Barry's Bay, Ontario. It was shipped to Warsaw. The two egg-shaped stones were the basis of the twin-pillar monument which bears the following inscription:

**"THESE TWO STONES
ONE FROM CANADA AND ONE FROM POLAND
COMMEMORATE THE CANADIAN AND POLISH SOLDIERS
WHO FOUGHT SIDE BY SIDE
DURING THE SECOND WORLD WAR"**

At a state dinner, the General who commanded the Polish Armoured Division, made reference to the 'white horse' incident. He suggested it was a tribute which allowed a high-ranking Polish cavalry officer, who had been captured on September 4 '39, to regain his honour. My small part in the entire episode was recognized by the Polish Minister of Defence. How? By awarding me a medal. It marks my modest contribution to an episode which gave the Poles an even greater appreciation of the friendly cooperation which allowed both the Polish and the Canadian divisions, en route to close the Falaise Gap, to work in harmony and develop a great friendship.

Chapter 33

EMILE - - THE SNIPER

No easy hopes or lies
Shall bring us to our goal
But iron sacrifice
Of body, will, and soul.
There is but one task for all –
One life for each to give.
Who stands if Freedom fall?

Rudyard Kipling

RFN EMILE GENEST knew he was good at what he did. He was fearless. He told me he was happy in battle.

EMILE GENEST was noticed in his platoon. Even though he had reached the age of 20 and still looked like a beardless youth, he had qualities which endeared him to his comrades in the Rifles. His main skill was the manner in which he handled a sniper's rifle. Like its German counterpart, the remodelled Canadian version was also a superb weapon. It had a hair-trigger and the best telescope, with cross-hairs, which had been crafted by armament experts. At 300 yards, **EMILE GENEST'S** aim was deadly and a legend grew around him. He had been personally responsible for 'knocking off' at least 10 Germans in the village of Grafjan, which was considered middle ground. The Leopold Canal was the border between Belgium and Holland and formed the Southern boundary of the Breskens Pocket between the Canal itself and the Scheldt Estuary on the North. **EMILE** occupied an ideal position for a sniper. It was near the ruins of a cement casement. We had taken it over as Headquarters of CHARLIE Company which was under my command.

EMILE sent back a message, calling for more ammunition. While we waited for the CSM to bring up the steel-nosed bullets, I had an opportunity to chat with him. An interesting story emerged. He told me he was born near Spearhill, a small French-speaking Manitoba community and was the youngest of 14 children.

Our snipers were carried on the strength of the Intelligence platoon. Generally they had their own specialties, collectively a great bunch in their own right.

In addition to his expertise as a sharpshooter, EMILE spoke fluent French. This meant he could communicate with many of the new reinforcements. They came up to the RWR as a result of PRIME MINISTER MACKENZIE KING'S decision to release some 16,000 well-trained home defence troops, being held back in Canada for whatever reason. As well, he could speak with the French and many of the Belgian civilians whose assistance on our trek from France to Holland was invaluable.

EMILE GENEST was killed on October 10 '44 at the Leopold Canal when he was only 20 years of age. He was wounded in a one-on-one battle with a crack German marksman; one of a handful of superb SS snipers who had been left behind in a 'safe nest' when his group was retreating northward and to the east from the Breskens Pocket. The German sharpshooters were part of a small 'rearguard' group whose mission was to protect their comrades who were in full flight. The remnants of Hitler's forces were attempting to cross from Breskens on the North West shore of the Scheldt, across the wide entrance to Flushing. If the German soldiers succeeded, they would trek across Walcheren Island in a wild dash for the Rhine and their homeland.

EMILE'S brother had joined the Cameron Highlanders of Winnipeg. He was particularly disturbed when he heard of EMILE'S death. After visiting his body he gave us more information on the fascinating EMILE. Asked where he had learned to shoot, the brother told us the secret of EMILE'S prowess with a weapon that demanded a good eye and steady nerves. Near their farmhouse in Ashern, Manitoba, the major sport of the Genest boys in winter was snowball fights. EMILE, although the youngest, had by far the best throwing arm and a 'good eye.' According to his brother, this accounted for his accuracy at pinning down an adversary in a sniper's duel years later in the North West Europe campaign.

The policy in the Canadian Army was that an older brother could request a transfer of a younger brother. Using this procedure, the older brother had put in a request for EMILE to join the Camerons. By this time, EMILE was well settled in the Rifles. The request for transfer was somehow reshuffled and **EMILE** stayed with the RWR instead of transferring to his brother's unit.

The policy which must have been drafted by some chair-borne staff officer about 'brothers claiming brothers' was a fool's paradise. It was based on the assumption that an older brother could look after his more junior sibling. Usually the policy worked in reverse. The General staff wouldn't know that they had created a nightmare. The **EMILE GENEST** case is proof that the ill-conceived system was not effective. The grief shown by the older brother when he came up to our unit and saw the body of young **EMILE** meant that the Canadian Army could easily have lost two soldiers – **EMILE** to a sniper, and the older brother, who might have been overcome with grief to the point that his effectiveness was impaired.

Arrangements were made for **EMILE'S** brother to attend a temporary funeral on our side of the Leopold Canal. It was a scenario no one should have to witness – an older brother tending to the burial of his 'kid' brother who was the youngest in a family of 14.

If there is a positive side to the **GENEST** story it lies in the fact that the younger brother was a crack shot. Even before his 21st birthday he had the opportunity of killing what turned out to be 12 of the best snipers that the fleeing German SS could leave behind.

EMILE GENEST represented the very best that the Canadian Army had – he was bilingual, knew exactly what he was doing, and even at 20 had become a 'boy wonder' among his older fellow soldiers. The fact that he had brought an end to the harassment of at least 12 German snipers indicates the kind of soldier Emile was.

He is buried in the Adegem Military Cemetery in Belgium. He was the son of Ludger and Clara Genest. In choosing a geographical feature, *Genest Island* (63 1/2) lies in the Mishepowistik Lake, a hard place to find in that this unpronounceable name is one of 15 or 20 small lakes about 30 miles directly North from Lake Winnipeg – the largest body of fresh water in Central Manitoba.

POST-SCRIPT: The RWRs were among the first Canadian troops to capture the flushing casement at the Western tip of Walchern Island. **BERT FRASER**, the RWR intelligence officer, counted some 12 Germans who could have been laid to rest by the sniping skills of **EMILE GENEST** and his snipers. Most of the Germans had developed extensive sniping skills in the ruins of Stalingrad. Their average age was about 30. It is a matter of conjecture as to how the German snipers would have felt, had they known that they were up against a 20 year old who learned his skills because he was the youngest out of a family of 14 – and could win snowball fights.

Chapter 34

TO YOU WITH FAILING HANDS...

LEOPOLD CANAL

We may find on the pathway side, or the glintering flint,
Or other things so small and unregarded :
Descry far windows fired with the sun, to whom
Nothing is small or mean,
To us let the war be a leering ghost now shriven

Edmund Blunden

It has been part of the military tradition for centuries that no wounded soldier would be left on the battlefield. Every soldier knew the drill – if wounded, get him to the medics; if dead, bring back his body, if possible.

This ancient, unwritten law of the fighting man was displayed in a remarkable manner by **SGT DON MCGEACHIE** of Charlie Company.

The battle of the Leopold Canal is inscribed on the metal cap badge of the RWRs. The yeoman work of **DON MCGEACHIE** had much to do with this. Students of military history can point to many war heroes who are known for individual exploits.

I use the following example of **SGT SMOKEY SMITH** to point out the courage shown by individual soldiers such as **SGT DON MCGEACHIE**. The story of what he did at the Leopold Canal is, to use an overworked phrase, 'the stuff of legend.'

SMOKEY SMITH, VC of Vancouver, BC, is a prime example. It is a matter of great pride that I consider him a personal friend. On a visit to Italy, **SMOKEY** and I set out to find the location where he won his VC as a Private. It was at a crossing of the Savio River in Northern Italy. **SMOKEY'S** citation reads as follows:

> 'In Italy on the night of 21st-22nd October 1944, a Canadian Infantry Brigade was ordered to establish a bridgehead across the Savio River.

The Seaforth Highlanders of Canada were selected as the spearhead of the attack, and in weather most unfavourable to the operation they crossed the river and captured their objective in spite of strong opposition from the enemy.

Torrential rain had caused the Savio River to rise six feet in five hours, and as the soft vertical banks made it impossible to bridge the river no tanks or anti-tank guns could be taken across the raging stream to the support of the rifle companies.

As the right forward company was consolidating its objective it was suddenly counter-attacked by a troop of three Mark V Panther tanks supported by two self-propelled guns and about thirty infantry and the situation appeared hopeless.

Under heavy fire from the approaching enemy tanks, Private Smith, showing great initiative and inspiring leadership, led his P.I.A.T.(1) Group of two men across an open field to a position from which the P.I.A.T. could best be employed. Leaving one man on the weapon, Private Smith crossed the road with a companion and obtained another P.I.A.T. Almost immediately an enemy tank came down the road firing its machine-guns along the line of the ditches. Private Smith's comrade was wounded. At a range of thirty feet and having to expose himself to the full view of the enemy, Private Smith fired the P.I.A.T. and hit the tank, putting it out of action. Ten German infantry immediately jumped off the back of the tank and charged him with Schmeissers and grenades. Without hesitation Private Smith moved out on the road and with his Tommy gun at point-blank range, killed four Germans and drove the remainder back. Almost immediately another tank opened fire and more enemy infantry closed in on Smith's position. Obtaining some abandoned Tommy gun magazines from a ditch, he steadfastly held his position, protecting his comrade and fighting the enemy with his Tommy gun until they finally gave up and withdrew in disorder.

One tank and both self-propelled guns had been destroyed by this time, but yet another tank swept the area with fire from a longer range. Private Smith, still showing utter contempt for enemy fire, helped his wounded friend to cover and obtained medical aid for him behind a nearby building. He then returned to his position beside the road to await the possibility of a further enemy attack.

No further immediate attack developed, and as a result the battalion was able to consolidate the bridgehead position so vital to the success of the whole operation, which led to the capture of San Giorgio Di Cesena and a further advance to the Ronco River.

Thus, by the dogged determination, outstanding devotion to duty and superb gallantry of this private soldier, his comrades were so inspired that the bridgehead was held firm against all enemy attacks, pending the arrival of tanks and anti-tank guns some hours later.'

SMOKEY SMITH will be the first to tell you that the ranks of the Canadian Army contained many tough, brilliant, fearless soldiers whose contribution to the defeat of the Germans were equal to his. There is room for disagreement. The courage and the tactical advantage gained by the Canadians, in respect of the action for which **SMOKEY** received his VC, stands very high on the list for which this honour has been created. Incidentally, it is a cardinal principle of the British Government, responsible for awarding VCs, that the courage shown in any citation would not be ranked in comparison with other VCs. Having said this, many will agree that **SMOKEY'S** single-handed action against the German attackers certainly cannot be equalled by the exploits of many other VC winners – no matter how deserving they may be.

Not one to argue with my friend **SMOKEY**, I will simply take his word for it – at the same time pointing out what **DON MCGEACHIE** did at the Leopold Canal. **DON** was an old timer with the Winnipeg Rifles. He enlisted during the first week we mobilized. He literally fought and scrabbled his way up the ranks from private soldier to sergeant. The Leopold Canal scrap was in October of 1944. By this time, **DON MCGEACHIE** had become another of the stalwart non-commissioned officers upon whom this battalion counted heavily.

The episode which is best remembered from the Leopold Canal Battle concerns **Lt Jim Kerr**, who was in command of a platoon of Charlie Company which crossed the Leopold Canal the night of October 7 '44.

The crossing was after dark. The lighting was provided by the flamethrowers mounted on the carriers, and slanted upwards at a 45-degree angle.

The first of a number of segments in the **McGeachie** story commenced when we took a 60-hundredweight truck back to B Echelon to pick up reinforcements. **Don** was in the back. We loaded up the 'new boys.' At the first stop, **Don** came around to the passenger side and told me that the reinforcements were all French-speaking. What are we going to do about that? This was the first time that the infamous conscription issue had hit our battalion. Earlier that week, **Prime Minister Mackenzie King** had released some 16,000 Home Defence troops for overseas service.

Incidentally, they had been hoodwinked into Articles of Conscription, in probably the lowest form of treatment. The conscription form contained two very offensive provisions.

The first was that those being conscripted would have the 'privilege' of the defence of Great Britain. Many of the conscripts were of French-Canadian origin. They had ample reason to be critical of the British who, at the Plains of Abraham under **Gen James Wolfe**, had defeated French **Gen Montcalm**. This battle, irrespective of the consequences – good or bad – resulted in Britain taking possession of Canada from the French. No 'credit' was given to the fact that France had done much to settle the country with farmers, trappers and other white men, sometimes against the well-documented wishes of the native population.

The second offensive provision was that they could be sent overseas, but most of them had signed the English form – hence they did not understand the commitment.

So much for the conscription issue. It had practically split Canada apart on a number of occasions – including participation of the Canadian Expeditionary Force in World War I. A second development was a repetition of the disruption in World War II. For the purposes of this writing, however, we can leave the matter to be sorted out by others.

Getting back to **DON MCGEACHIE**, he solved the French-English dilemma in the good old Canadian way. Many would call it compromise. We went to the back of the 60-hundredweight and asked into the darkness if any of the soldiers could speak English. One French-Canadian said that he could. We told him to jump down and, on my own, I immediately promoted him to corporal. His name was **BOB CROUSSETTE**.

We had a truckload of very nervous soldiers who had been transported in the dark, up to the Leopold Canal. The area was alive with shellfire, flamethrowers, small arms bullets and mortar bombs. They wondered, quite naturally, where they were. I had to jump back into the front to show the driver the road up to the Leopold Canal. **SGT MCGEACHIE** – a commanding figure – clambered into the 60-hundredweight. His hobnailed boots were stomping around. He did remember a few words of high school French.

MCGEACHIE soon realized that the reinforcement troops, fresh from Valcartier training camp in Canada, were a bit uneasy. No amount of French or English would settle them down. It was time for **MCGEACHIE** to put on his act. He cleared the middle of the corrugated metal floor and gave his best imitation of a very disturbed NCO – which he was.

We reached the canal. Matters were confused. It was pitch dark, but exploding star shells gave off an eerie source of light. We had originally crossed the canal in Kapok and Canvas Boats. These were of the folding variety. They could be carried by two men and would hold up to eight while in the water.

By this time, our pioneer platoon had scrounged enough material to install a floating footbridge. It was pitch black now. We could find neither the boats nor the footbridge. Also, no one really knew at that stage the depth of the Leopold Canal. Finally, **MCGEACHIE** found three of the original flimsy assault boats.

The new French-speaking recruits were quick to conclude that if they did not join **MCGEACHIE**, they would be left on the RWR side of the canal, which was under very heavy fire. It did not take long for the boats to be filled up. Also, the Rifles pioneer platoon under **LT BILL SPEECHLEY** had re-located the Kapok bridge. What **MCGEACHIE** had done so far on this evening comes under the heading of 'leadership' in a very big way. Once we were on the German side of the raised bank of the Leopold Canal, MCGEACHIE took over. He had a phenomenal memory for where the Germans had previously dug, what the Americans called, 'foxholes.' Our French-Canadian friends wanted protection from the shelling, and it took all of two minutes for MCGEACHIE to get the new conscripts under safe cover. He was their hero from that point on.

As daylight broke on October 10 '44, I received some bad news. LT JIMMY KERR had been a friend of mine since the mobilization of the battalion. He came from Saint Vital, Manitoba, where I had lived at one time. MCGEACHIE came to me – the only word that could describe his mood was solemnity. I knew something was wrong. He pointed to a brown lump in a flooded polder field. It was a body. He then told me that I was looking at my long-time friend, JIMMY KERR … and he would go get the 'remains' for a burial.

What made the episode more poignant was that, the night before, Jimmy and I sat and polished off a bottle of rum. JIMMY had seen a great deal of action by this time. He told me very seriously that he had the feeling that he would 'get it' the next day. This fact did not help matters any.

When we talk of coincidences like this, I am reminded of a comment sometimes attributed to Mark Twain: "Truth is stranger than fiction." Only LT KERR and I know what JIMMY said to me the night before the Leopold battle. It can be believed or not. As JIM was killed the next day, I am the only one who could testify to his feeling that the war would catch up with him.

SGT MCGEACHIE saw my concern. Just then a message came through from the CO, ordering me to take a patrol up to the village of Grafjan, which ran along a rough road at a 90-degree angle north from the canal bank. JIM KERR's death devastated me. MCGEACHIE saw this. He looked at me and said "Don't worry, sir, I'll take the attack in." I refused and, using the ditches, took off for Grafjan.

The road ran about 600 yards. We laid down smoke but the wind dissipated it. The wily Germans let us run in the clear of a bright sunlit day for about 350 yards. Then they opened fire. We had seven casualties. MCGEACHIE, still leading a charmed life, practically pushed me back to my bunker, then began personally dragging our own wounded out of enemy fire. I was later told that he had saved four badly wounded soldiers. Then was killed.

That was the same afternoon upon which I received my final wound. It is not difficult to imagine my feelings when I saw two private soldiers dragging **McGeachie** into our bunker. He was badly wounded. He died on October 12 '44 at 26 years of age. I make it a point to visit his grave in Adegem Military Cemetery in Belgium whenever I have the opportunity.

His permanent geographical feature, named by the Manitoba Government, is *McGeachie Lake* (64 O/1), east of Munroe Lake. There should be a marker saying 'THIS LAKE IS NAMED IN HONOUR OF A GALLANT SOLDIER - - ONE OF THE BEST!'

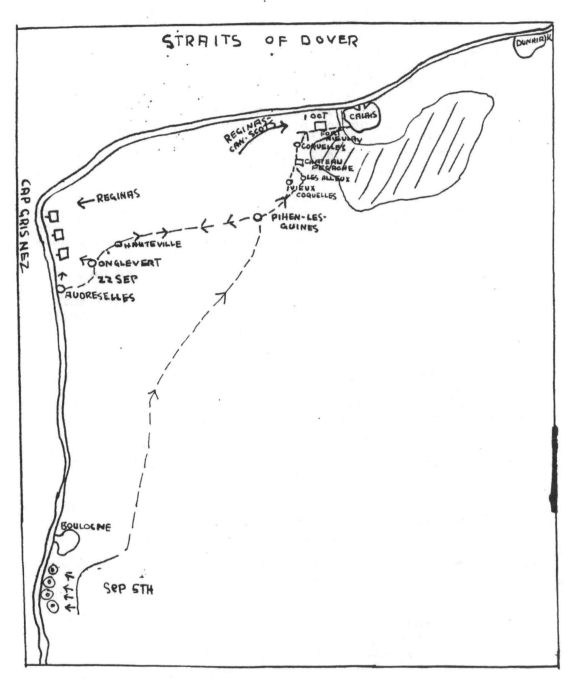

STRAITS OF DOVER

DUNKIRK

CAP GRIS NEZ

CALAIS

1 OCT

REGINAS-
CAN. SCOTS

FORT
NIEULAY

← REGINAS

COQUELLES

CHATEAU
PECACHE

LES ALLEUX

VIEUX
COQUELLES

PIHEN-LES-
GUINES

HAUTEVILLE

ONGLEVERT
22 SEP

AUDRESELLES

BOULOGNE

SEP 5TH

CALAIS AREA

Chapter 35

ATTEMPTED AMBUSH

You're walking on the fightin' side of me
Runnin' down the way of life
That fightin' men have fought and died to keep
Let this song I'm singin' be a warnin'
If you're runnin' down my country, man
You're walkin' on the fightin' side of me

Merle Haggard

The following episode tells the story of how the Canadians, after a little battle experience, handled themselves.

Apparently, a German Commander came across some members of the RWR anti-tank and mortar platoons, more-or-less at rest. The Germans were planning an attack when a nasty but foolhardy SS trooper, aged just over 20, boasted that he could bring back the whole group of Canadians – and do it single-handedly.

The German Commandant needed information from the RWRs. He did not want to throw cold water on the bold plan of his single SS Hitler youth ... besides, he was short-handed.

In order to keep his sneak attack as quiet as possible, the lone German SS apparently said he would take only one grenade. He decided to sneak up on these RWR specialists who were engaged in a 'bull session.'

He crawled close to the guys of the mortar and anti-tank crew who were sitting around relaxing. He was probably showing off to his comrades but panicked and threw his one grenade into the middle of the RWR gang.

It landed on the lap of an RWR in the group, by the name of **JACK PARKS**. **BUTCH MULHAUSEN**, a seasoned veteran by now, without breaking into a sweat, chucked the grenade back in the direction of the retreating German. By this time the tape on the handle of the grenade unwound. This was the defence mechanism in this type of grenade which would go off only if thrown so the tape could come loose.

Another one of the battle hardened Winnipegs by the name of **PETE ENNS** (who was a bit of a clown) saw that the Jerry had been felled by his own grenade and sang a popular song at that time. The punch line was 'So long, it's been good to know you.' Then they got up, saw that they could nothing for the German so covered him with his smock and left him to be retrieved by his own kind.

This is by way of introducing the kind of Canadian soldier that the humourless German would never understand. **PETE ENNS** was often called Hop-along Cassidy because of his striking resemblance to the western movie star. **'HOPPY' ENNS** went right along with the gag and developed the same easygoing drawl and chuckle which many had laughed at while watching B movies at the neighbourhood movie houses back home.

PETE was a damn good soldier. One of the tricks he taught himself, to go along with the Hop-along caricature, was to crack a bull-whip with deadly accuracy – much to the 'enjoyment' of some Jerry onlookers who had deserted to our side as a safe way out of the war.

Prior to enlistment, **ENNS** was in the cattle business. Germans could never fully understand how a happy-go-lucky 27 year old with a bent for mimicking a well-known Hollywood cowboy actor would join a war across the Atlantic Ocean.

The circumstances which led to **PETE ENN'S** enlistment are quoted here verbatim: "I was on a cattle train from Edmonton, looking after cattle, all the way to Winnipeg. The only accommodation in the 'Peg was in the cattle cars. I did not have time to clean up so I nestled down with a few Holsteins. The temporary bedmates made things somewhat uncomfortable, to say nothing of the odour."

Finally, without sleep, **ENNS** walked outside the main CNR station in Winnipeg. Fortunately (or perhaps not) he ran into **CSM NELS BUHR** who was supervising an enlistment office for the Rifles. **NELS** had been a policeman in the tough North End of Winnipeg. He could handle any situation. He immediately signed up **PETE** 'for the duration.'

The long and the short of it is that one handshake in the vice-like grip of **NELS** and the deed was done. That is to say **PETE ENNS** became an RWR.

PETE'S friends in Normandy had a good laugh in telling (let's call him Hoppy) episodes. Probably the most famous was when **PETE**, after his first wound was, as he put it, 'shuffled off under protest' to the French-speaking Chaudière Regiment.

To the staff officers in charge of reinforcements, it was the 'sergeant' stripes on **HOPPY'S** arm that was the big attraction, despite the fact that he spoke no French. Good sergeants were in short supply, no matter whether they could speak the language.

The next part of the tale is again in **PETE ENNS** own words: "One night they sent us on a patrol. It was hell. The French Canadian guys (fearless no doubt) kept chatting away in their native tongue and would not listen to a new English-speaking Sergeant." **PETE** recognized the danger of this situation if patrolling was to continue. Next day, he paraded himself to the Chaudière's Company Commander. As he put it: "In a few hours I was on my way back to the Rifles."

PETE ENNS survived the war and moved out West where there was a happy and fast growing group of ex-RWR. He enjoyed the company of his son and, as he says, particularly 'the 19th hole on the Chemainus Golf Club.'

Those who saw **PETE ENNS** in action in Normandy tell the picture of 'a man who knew no fear.' He was a born leader. Men would follow him anywhere. They trusted him. Moreover, he had a photographic memory for map references. Without them, it was all too easy to become lost in the maze of sunken roads, hedge roads, farm buildings and shell-holes that were the battleground before Falaise was captured.

Back to the attempted ambush. It is interesting to try to understand the thoughts of the hapless German who had come across a nonchalant bunch of anti-tank and mortar men, lounging around their equipment. He sensed an easy time of taking them prisoners. When he panicked, he tossed a grenade into the lap of the Canadians. **BUTCH** coolly flipped the grenade back at the retreating German. It exploded, which ended Fritz's war there and then. This gives some idea of the kind of boys that made up the Canadian divisions in Normandy.

Lady luck seemed to favour the anti-tank platoon. The gang mentioned above included **JACK PARKS** who became an officer and was transferred to the British Army. **BUTCH MULHAUSEN** and **PETE ENNS** survived the war and remained close friends for the rest of their lives.

Chapter 36

OVERHEARD AT THE MOBILE BATH

With regard to excellence, it is not enough to know, but we must try to have and use it.

Aristotle

After 54 continuous days in action since D-Day, the Regiment was sent to a Rest Area near Deauville on the Channel coast. As we travelled into a large field, we saw several 30-hundredweight trucks loaded with huge tanks. Running from them were pipes carrying water. Holes had been drilled into the pipes at irregular intervals. It was a rough type of shower. This was the infamous mobile bath arrangement. A soldier, upon entering, took off his clothes and walked into the cold water streaming from the punctured hose. As he left, he would pick up his clean clothing and go back to the battalion area where tents were allocated for sleeping purposes.

There was always a line-up so, on this particular afternoon, we sat around shooting the breeze. The conversation got around to who was the best soldier in the RWR. The hands-down choice was **RSM Mickey Austin**. Talk also centred around who would be at the other end of the spectrum – that is, the worst soldier. No one could or would come up with a name. Then **Joe Sakolinski** ambled into view. There was an inclination to say that he would qualify as the worst. Then we recalled his acts of courage in the face of the enemy. We agreed that **Joe** looked like 'the runt of the litter' as he was the most unkempt, however, he had earned the reputation as being a fire-eating soldier.

RSM Mickey Austin

One day at our camp in England, **Mickey Austin**, a smart-looking RSM from the Permanent Force, showed up. He leaped from his jeep at the guard's quarters and lined up the sleepy-looking, bedraggled sentries. He inspected every one of them. His tirade ended by telling them that they were shaming the King's uniform. An auspicious start!

MICKEY AUSTIN proved to be one of those rare birds. He went by the book in matters of dress. As an NCO in battle, however, he won a Military Cross – a gallantry decoration usually awarded only to commissioned officers.

At first blush, MICKEY was none too popular with the troops. Their opinion rose from what was known as his 'regimental attitude,' no doubt developed when MICKEY was in the Regular Forces before the war. Incidentally, there was a well known saying among Canadian Troops at that time. It was that we were fighting two enemies: number <u>one</u> were the Germans; a close <u>second</u> were the Canadians who had been part of the PERMANENT FORCE, many of whom brought an atmosphere of disdain at having to work with civilians in uniform.

MICKEY soon overcame any arrogance he may have brought with him. The O/Rs began to recognize that a good RSM needed to maintain some aloofness. They accepted him because, beneath his haughty demeanor, he was a great guy to have around. He also straightened out a few questionable junior officers which, incidentally, was the RSM's job!

As a group of rough and ready civilians, we realized we would need some military skills if we were to take on the German SS. MICKEY AUSTIN drilled those skills into the Rifles until they became second nature. It couldn't be said that the men loved him, but he certainly had their respect.

An illustration of how MICKEY impressed the ordinary guys occurred on the road toward Soulangy. We were on the move, en route to close the gap between Caen and Falaise. MICKEY, in a Jeep, came barrelling along. A luckless Canadian lieutenant jumped out of a slit trench, wondering about the fuss. An American Mustang fighter had crashed earlier. MICKEY had taken off the .50-calibre machine gun and mounted it on the hood of his jeep. His pastime ... 'let's find some Germans' even though he knew he was attracting enemy snipers by exposing himself. As proof of his contempt for the enemy, there were bullet holes in his windshield. He had already been at work.

He addressed the young officer, suggesting he jump in the back of the jeep to find out if he passed muster in MICKEY'S eyes. The officer said he couldn't leave his platoon. MICKEY looked at him and shook his head, in obvious disgust.

The .50-calibre was loaded with high explosive ammo. Looking down the road, **Mickey** spotted a possible nest of German machine-gunners. He drove into a farmyard. He then took seven or eight POW's after killing a few 'die hard' Nazis who were spoiling for a scrap.

With men like **Mickey**, there was no problem in deciding who our 'best soldier' was.

Joe Sakolinski

Here was a soldier you would want on your side as well. **Joe Sakolinski** was one of those tough little guys that populated the Canadian Infantry. He despised the German Nazi 'supermen.' He enlisted from behind a store counter in Brandon, Manitoba. He was Jewish and he was out to settle a score.

It was July 8 '44. Perched on a hill, **Joe** was watching Caen being bombed by the RAF the night before the 3rd Brigade was supposed to capture this large city in Northern France.

Joe's comments would not find space in a family newspaper. In fact, every time an Allied bomb hit Caen, **Joe** had real trouble in restraining his joy.

Joe suddenly went quiet. He was on his back, gazing at the sky. Two Lancaster bombers of the RAF or RCAF were in flames, hit by anti-aircraft flak. They were plummeting down close to our vantage point. What was going through **Joe Sakolinski's** mind? It was one thing to bomb the German defenders in Caen. It was another thing to think that this was costing the lives of Bomber Command crews.

This was not the first time **Joe** had viewed an enemy bombardment. On D plus 4, the unit was dug in near the village of Putot-en-Bessin. **Joe** was acting as a runner. The radio was acting up. **Joe** was told to get a message back to the Air Liaison Officer (ALO) at RWR battalion headquarters. This was serious business. There was a concentration of Germans forming up about 250 yards south of the Caen-Bayeux railroad tracks.

The RWR was under shellfire. **JOE** jumped out of his slit trench (the Yanks called them foxholes, by the way). He ran like a madman, zig zagging among the other RWR. The only way to reach our tactical headquarters was on foot ... a dodgy job, the Limeys would say.

Four shells landed close to **JOE**. The ground lit up and **JOE** yelled in defiance, still on the run. Fifteen minutes went by. **JOE** had returned to his slit trench.

No one believed that **JOE'S** message would get through. Minutes later, **JOE** saw some RAF Typhoon bombers paste the area where the Germans had concentrated.

Outside of the assault on Juno Beach, this was the greatest day of **JOE SAKOLINSKI**'s life.

Incidentally, **JOE** established himself as a favourite with the guys during the early days of training in Camp Shilo. A full battalion parade was in progress. **JOE'S** platoon was breaking in a new officer who had all the signs of becoming a pain in the derrière ... volunteering the platoon for extra duties and all that jazz. This officer was standing in his proper place, all alone, 20 yards in front of his men who were lined up in columns of three. The CO gave the order for a RIGHT TURN. The officer turned LEFT. **JOE** yelled out for all to hear – YOUR ARMY RIGHT ... adding sarcastically, SIR. **JOE** made a lot of new friends in the platoon that day. Someone said 'quite a guy.' They were right.

Chapter 37

FORT NIEULAY

The best victory is when the opponent surrenders
of its own accord before there are any actual hostitilies . . .
It is best to win without fighting.

Sun-tzu (400 BC)

Those of us who were old enough to be in uniform in World War II will doubtlessly remember this scenario. On most Tuesday evenings, during the 'dirty thirties,' we would gather around the family radio to listen to a popular broadcast of the time. The star was **BARON MUNCHAUSEN** – a man who has gone down in literary history as the world's greatest liar.

It was his forte to tell the most ridiculous tales. (I still remember one. It was about a man who ran across a frozen roadway in the dark and was cut to pieces by the beams from a car's headlights.)

When questioned about the veracity of his tale, **MUNCHAUSEN** came up with surely one of the funniest lines in radio. In broken German, he would say: "Vas you dere, Sharlie?" It brought immediate closure.

The story of **BARON MUNCHAUSEN** is appropriate. In checking official histories of the Rifles at Fort Nieulay, the researchers mangled the truth so badly that the famous "Vas you dere, Sharlie?" comes to mind.

It was known from French sympathizers who were familiar with the Fort, that its walls contained intricate tunnels.

The necessity lay in having to get into the Fort and rout the defenders from their rabbit warrens. Despite the intelligence reports from the French Maquis (members of the Resistance), there were many German troops obviously being readied to block the area against an Allied force which might attempt to occupy or bypass Calais.

The chroniclers who wrote about Fort Nieulay after the war were not there. The RWRs were!

The incident at Fort Nieulay cost the lives of Canadians, but it did have its comical moments. The Fort was built centuries ago as part of the defences of the city of Calais. Its ramparts housed guns meant to repel invasion from either the sea or the land. Not so strange. An invader could land elsewhere on the coast and mount an attack from the rear. In September '44, Fort Nieulay lay directly in the path of the 7th Brigade of the Canadian 3rd Division which was doggedly fighting its way eastward with the English Channel on its left.

Nieulay is memorialized in the history of the RWRs. One of the Regiment's battle honours is emblazoned on its cap badge. This emphasizes the importance of this battlement which stood in the way of the capture of Calais.

The main objective of capturing the Fort itself was left to the RWRs. The lay of the land is important. The whole northern coast of France was the brainchild of **GERMAN GEN ERWIN ROMMEL**. The Western approaches to Calais were guarded by huge guns mounted in four enormous concrete bunkers. For two years, these guns had been firing very heavy shells across the English Channel at Folkeston and Dover. The German fortifications, called Cap Gris Nez, could be approached from the village of Audrecelles in France, lying a mile or so inland. German prisoners said that their commander, aware of the hopelessness of his situation, would readily surrender.

The CO of Dog Company at the time was **MAJ LOCKIE FULTON**. He asked for volunteers to approach the Cap Gris Nez command post. Despite the well-worn adage that one should never volunteer for anything during wartime, the idea got the better of me. My CSM, **JIM SHARPE** and his driver, **AL FERRIER**, agreed to accompany me. Up the crude road to the main casement we went in a jeep, with a white bed sheet flying.

We came to a barbed-wire gate. The German guard, obviously with permission from on high, allowed us in.

When we reached Command Headquarters, an arrogant SS officer came out. He spoke no English but his attitude needed no interpretation. He had his guards take us down three flights of stairs. Enough German came to mind for me to warn the ruthless Commandant all about the Geneva Conventions, and the consequences if he proceeded with his all-too-obvious intent.

He had called out a firing party, but thought better of it. He waved his hand in disgust and said probably the only appropriate words that came to mind: "Vamoose – Schnell."

If there is a record for climbing three flights of concrete stairs, it belonged to me. **JIMMY SHARP** and **AL FERRIER** were running a close second, but that was because I was blocking their way. We jumped in the jeep and re-traced our vehicle tracks down the hillside. The German commander had second thoughts about letting us go. We heard shots zinging off our jeep. This was the overture to the taking of Fort Nieulay.

The RWR, who were there, tell the real story of what happened at the Fort. The area was to be bombed by Lancasters. Unfortunately cloud cover presaged what might have been a real debacle for the occupants. The Lancasters returned to England with their bomb loads.

Next came a set piece attack on this huge fortress. The outer defences proved impenetrable. Darkness was approaching. Our CO, recognizing the potential losses to his men, wisely called a halt. Tomorrow would give time to work out a new plan.

After some serious scouting, we saw that the condition of the huge doors past the moat showed years of rot. This called for a carrier assault.

SGT JOE ROSHICK commanded the lead vehicle, with fire spouting from its flamethrowers. **LT GORDON EMBURY** led some Winnipeg Rifles on foot.

ROSHICK crossed the moat and smashed in the burning wooden doors. They collapsed and in we went.

The German Commander's quarters were spotted inside. The communications line to German HQ in Calais was still functioning! A field telephone jangled when the wheel which ran the generator was rotated by handle. From the other end: "Ja?"

We rustled up a German-speaking Canadian. He warned that if the Fort did not surrender, it would be bombed into submission. The news spread. Scared Germans streamed out, gathering in the parade ground in the centre of the Fort. They held various white rags with their hands in the air. The prisoners were never really counted, but at least 300 would be fairly accurate.

JOE ROSHICK, who had a well-earned reputation as a scrounger, lined up the surrendering Germans. They were relieved of any valuables. One despondent Nazi turned over the prisms and other instruments of magnification from X-ray machines. Valuable loot, indeed! He had been raiding medical facilities for weeks as the Germans retreated.

The ground attack which finally secured the entrance earned LT GORDON EMBURY a Military Cross. JOE ROSHICK was awarded a Military Medal. The author (me) was later granted the French Legion of Honour for stilling the Cap Gris Nez guns. Their huge projectiles could point not only at the England coast 20 miles away, but could be turned inward. We saw one shell, fired at a French village, completely demolish a small group of farm buildings and a church.

Where does BARON Munchausen come in? Reading from the official history of the RWRs, we extract the following quotes:

> *Although 9500 prisoners were taken, the Canadian casualties numbered 634.*

> *Newly appointed divisional commander, Major-General D.C. Spry, in planning the attack on Fort Nieulay, called on an unusual combination of artillery fire to open the battle.*

Note: The Fort actually was taken by one carrier crew which burned down the wooden door to gain entry. Vas you dere General? I vas! So vas LT. EMBURY UND ROSHICK.

Again, quoting from the RWR history:

> *"While the heavy guns of his artillery opened fire from landward side, even mightier guns of the Royal Navy shelled the defences from the sea and from*

far-off Dover on the other side of the Channel, the biggest guns of all joined in."

So much for the armchair historians.

Again from the history:

"At 1000 hours the Rifles left their start line, following the artillery barrage. ... Another point identified on the map as Vieux Coquelles presented more difficulties."

All of the guns, even those of the Royal Navy from its ships in the Channel, had little to do with the taking of the Fort. That was accomplished by some determined RWR and a one tracked vehicle – its fire produced by flamethrowers.

The generals knew little of how the fort was taken. Did they do their research? As for me, "I vas dere, Sharlie."

Inside the Fort, the ragged group of prisoners were lined up in single file (**CSM CARL BROWN** called it a 'column of a lump'). **JOE ROSHICK** noted a fat, sloppily-dressed German administrative type struggling to hide in a stairwell. **JOE'S** eagle eye had spotted a walking treasure trove. He was right.

The overfed, beefy German – not surprisingly a paymaster – had stuffed among his baggy pants a storehouse of booty. Unfortunately, the fat German's pants gave way. Tinned food, liquor, Canadian watches and other valuables poured onto the parade square. Never one to let a golden opportunity pass by, the enterprising **ROSHICK** deftly clipped the belt from our SS paymaster. Again, success.

JOE SAKOLINSKI saw an opportunity to make up for some of the plunder taken from Jews consigned to the death camps. In his fragmented German, Joe gave the order for the German NCO to bend over. The seams in the rear end of the trousers parted. On view was a florid pink bum. Also more elite treasures such as rings, pearls and other indications of wealth spilled onto the pavement.

Somehow a Wittnauer silver wristwatch came into my possession. I couldn't find the owner. Yes ... I looked but thought it was made in USA (a city in Japan, I think). The watch served me for many a year.

Chapter 38

TONY – PART 2

Adversity does teach who your real friends are

Lois McMaster Bujold

Coincidence is often part of the battlefield. **TONY** (the Italian who worked on my Uncle's farm in England) landed in Normandy with the Green Howards. It was an unusual arrangement. It came about because **TONY** had been sent back from the desert as a POW by a British officer who kept in touch with his captive. When the Italian POWs were set free, **TONY** was allowed to serve in the British Army.

The RWR were near Elbeuf on the Seine River. **TONY** found out that our Regiment was occupying the town and his major brought him over in a jeep. Officers in the British Army, as a matter of military dictum, kept aloof from the other ranks. They can and do, however, mix freely with their batmen (or menservants, if you like).

I knew that **CSM BILLY BIRD** was a duck hunter extraordinaire. He had spent much of his youth in the marshes in the area from Selkirk to Grassmere Ditch (the 'Firing Line' to the uninitiated). The area is beloved by Ducks Unlimited. It stretches from Lake Winnipeg westward to Lake Manitoba.

TONY wanted to meet my CSM. **BILLY BIRD** was more than willing. While on his visit to Elbeuf in France, **TONY** and **BILLY** had a great chat in some caves.

BILLY and **TONY** had much in common. They were indeed familiar with the jargon of the duck hunter (lead the duck at least two feet for every 20 yards in the direction in which the duck is flying, etc., etc.)

They expressed warm feelings for each other which came from their similar backgrounds. The 'weirdness' of it all struck me many years later. I attempted to contact **TONY** through the British High Commissioner. He had gone to Australia. The trail was cold.

In the playbook of those who became friends during the war, the name of **TONY** appears. The cryptic note in my diary says: "Good hunter; good companion; all-around good guy."

The essential part of this story is that eventually **TONY** was fighting with <u>our side</u> in Normandy. He was not the only former Italian soldier in the British Army either.

All of this exposes a situation about which little has been written. When the Canadians were first in Normandy, they saw the soldier in a grey-green uniform with a coal scuttle helmet, or the dreaded SS with their cloth forage caps. It was only natural to think of them as Germans. The Italian soldier was easily recognized by his 'Pee Pot' helmet and his light green uniform.

It was seldom understood that a significant number of the enemy soldiers against whom we were fighting were not Germans at all. They were 'foreign conscripts. Some had originally been in the Polish Army. A good many were French who had been taken into the Organisation Todt as slave labourers. When the German fortifications were finished, they found themselves in the hated German uniform. The iron discipline meant that they would either fight for the Germans, or be shot.

An example which gained notoriety was a Pole by the name of **JAN JESIONEK** who was a witness to the first shooting of Canadian prisoners on orders of **GEN WILLIAM MOHNKE**. This was at the Abbaye d'Ardenne. He was a Polish conscript. More about conscripts later.

Chapter 39

CONSCRIPTS

In war, there are no unwounded soldiers

José Narosky

The coincidence of the same soldier fighting in Normandy on two different sides was fairly common. Many had come from countries which were overrun by the German hordes. If permissible, many showed their willingness to join the Canadian Army as a means of evening the score. Among those deserting from the German forces were the French who wanted nothing better than to kill Germans and, of course, find their families. The opportunity to surrender from the Wehrmacht would permit the soldier to get out of combat. Those of us in frontline combat were slow to realize the situation.

At first glance, to us, a German soldier was an enemy. We had no opportunity to examine his pedigree. As some of the pseudo-Germans surrendered, they did so with a leaflet which offered them safe conduct. They were not trying to avoid further fighting! They had no love for Germany. Without any loss of dignity, they could surrender. Their reasons were no affair of ours. Some wanted to join the Canadian Army and many did.

All we really knew, when we first saw the Germans en masse, is that we were up against a tough, well-disciplined Army, either in their grey-green uniforms or in their battle smocks. It took some time to recognize that at the backs of these 'puppet' conscripts were vicious German SS officers or NCOs. The foreign vassals were forced to fight or be shot in the back. Or possibly their families were, in reality, hostages.

It is sad, 60 years later, to understand that we may have taken pride in wiping out a German machine gun post. Perhaps our feelings would have been less sanguine if we knew that some of the defenders were fighting against their will, and their sympathies lay on our side. This is the craziness of war – at least as it was in North West Europe in World War II.

One anecdote involves an unwilling soldier. An attack on the village of Soulangy was underway. It was a 'strong point' defending the main route from Caen to Falaise. **GENERAL SIMONDS** had the bright idea (that's a pun) of shining searchlights against the clouds so that his troops would be able to find their way.

Unexpectedly, a German jumped from a bridge - his hands held high. He was shouting "Kamerad" – the traditional German exclamation for those who wished to surrender. His superiors had given him a Mauser rifle and he was ordered to join a German squad fighting on the Eastern Front. He was taken prisoner by the Russians, who had formed an unhappy battalion of Prisoners of War. They were particularly useful because they could operate the German tanks (Tiger, Panther, Mark IV, etc.). They also were very familiar with the German small arms, including the Schmeisser and the Spandau MGs. We called our new prisoner **HANS**, thinking him to be a German. In actuality, he was a Pole in German uniform. Was he really 'one of ours?'

HANS' attitude on offering to surrender was possibly an indication that he had no love for the Germans. He turned out to be popular with most of our Charlie Company guys.

His first chore was to dig a trench, something we needed to heat the large food canisters.

In keeping with the promise that, at least in part, this memoir is light-hearted, the **HANS** episode is classic. Our Company cook said that the German conscript was acting strangely. In digging the trench for the large containers for cooking, he noted that the dimensions were roughly the same as his own body. He thought he was being asked to dig his own grave! After he found this wasn't true, he calmed down. **HANS** spent several weeks with the Company before we were forced to send him back to the POW cage.

As it was, a considerable amount of time was spent with Hans. As with **TONY THE ITALIAN** and **HANS THE POLE**, it was eerie to find that their boyhoods had not been too different from our own. They may have lain in bushes or in duck blinds – hunting ducks and geese for the next family meal. It is easy to visualize that any of them might well have been a boyhood friend back home.

Why the possibility of a friendship? The Poles, Germans and Northern Italians came from the same area. If either **HANS** or **TONY** had spent their boyhoods in the same geographical location as many RWR, how different could their pre-war lives have been? Many written about here were not Germans – but victims of the German military mind-set. When the original ranks of the Wehrmacht or SS were depleting, new manpower existed. The Germans knew most could be made to fight. Firm discipline would see to it. It should be remembered also that their families were waiting back home. The Gestapo would do the rest.

The purpose of this chapter begs some explanation. Firstly, most Canadians thought that in Normandy we were fighting the regular members of the Wehrmacht as well as the SS. It is not well known that often we were up against conscripts of other European parentage. Having been captured by the German Army then, were 'ready-made' cannon fodder for the Regular German Army. Men could be forced to shoot in any direction.

Also, the Germans had an eye to pick out those who, under duress, would make possible soldiers. These people were (to coin a word) 'trainable.' They were usually good shots and, like many Canadians, had spent much of their boyhood in the fields and rural areas of their native countries.

This memoir has mentioned **HANS**. Later **GERD** enters. He started his war in an Estonian uniform and ended up conscripted (and put into dangerous situations time after time) by the German SS. Some categories of unfortunate troops forced into German uniforms came from European countries taken over by **HITLER**. They had been utilized, under brutal conditions, to build German fortifications. Once their usefulness was obsolete for construction purposes, they were given two options: either fight with Germany as a reluctant soldier, or – we will leave the other circumstance to the imagination. As stated earlier, defenceless families left behind were at the mercy of those who could suffer if the foreigner in German uniform wouldn't fight for The Third Reich!

RECONCILIATION – A TOUGH QUESTION

This memoir talks about soldiers conscripted into the German Army whose sympathies lay elsewhere. This should not be seen as a proposal for reconciliation.

The belief is strong that only the victims can forgive. Very few victims are prepared to go this far.

The information regarding the other nationalities forced to fight for Germany is a matter of setting forth information which may not have been fully realized.

Chapter 40

BILLY BIRD

Sleep on, brave heart. Our cause is ours no longer
The world rolls on without our aid.
We fought for right, but hate and fear are stronger
We dreamed of peace, and dreams have been betrayed.

Edgar McInnis

A beautiful laneway runs west from the Château Pegache. It is a remarkable grove of beautiful trees – the like of which is seldom seen anywhere.

At the crest of the hill, toward the ancient old Château, nature again tried her very best. It became another set of ruins weakened by her long-time enemy – the explosives of modern war.

The terrible crimes which desecrated this small corner of France all those 60-odd years ago bring a lump to the throat.

It was September 25 '44. My infantry company was engaged in a fierce attack on Germans who occupied the Château.

A radio transmission had been sent back to our tactical HQ by my signaller. It was an urgent request for ammunition! **CSM BILL BIRD** answered the call. He swiftly gathered the supplies and was on his way. Through field glasses, he could be seen coming up the hill. He was standing up, guiding the carrier to make certain that no mines were run over. His diligence would see that no impediments stood in the way of the materiel of war which Charlie Company needed in order to take the Château or defend it against the expected German counter attack.

We froze. The unmistakable sound of a German sniper's rifle zinged through the air, piercing the duller sounds of the mortars. Horrified, we watched through the binoculars. **BILLY** crumpled forward. His battle was over. The German sniper who did the deed was in the branches of a tree along this beautiful laneway.

It is time, then, to reflect back to this despicable deed which took place on a sunny afternoon in September '44.

The needs of war take precedence. **BILL BIRD** knew that in the shadows at the Château Pegache we were engaged in a vicious firefight – MG bullets, grenades flung through the tree branches, German 88 shells doing their best to kill not only the Canadian attackers but even the German defenders.

When the Château was finally in our hands, we went looking for the German who had killed **BILL**. The sniper was found tied in the leafy branches of a tree. He descended at the command of the men of Charlie Company. They were in a foul mood. They had lost their beloved Sergeant Major in what appeared to be an act which could only be described as contemptible.

The German uniform-clad sniper hit the ground with his hands up, throwing away his sniper's rifle. It had a beautifully-tooled scope with crosshairs and a trigger mechanism which would, in all likelihood, ensure that the target was hit.

Where was the surprise? When the sniper raised his hands, he began to speak in a language none of us understood. He did, however, know some English and said that he was an Estonian.

RFN MIKE SZUMSKI, of our Intelligence Section, came forward. He could speak with the sniper in the Estonian language. He asked the guy, in Estonian, what he was doing in a German Army uniform. The circumstances were a bit tangled. The sniper, who looked to be about 30 years of age, told us that he had been working in the Russian shipyards and had been rounded up and mustered into the Russian Army in the defence of Stalingrad. In relating the man's story, **SZUMSKI** was adamant that his captive had no love for the Germans. He had, however, been captured in a Russian uniform along with a number of able-bodied men from his own village.

He gave a long account of having escaped from the Russian Army when the Germans had been defeated in Stalingrad and were fleeing eastward towards the Baltic region.

We called him **GERD** to make things simple. When we got to know him, we called him our 'quick change' expert but, he seemed to be sincere.

SZUMSKI got a little hot under the collar and said that he was suspicious as to how **GERD** got into the German Army. It had happened to many of those herded into the Russian Army for the defence of Stalingrad. When the Germans finally got to processing our friend **GERD**, he became an 'instant German.'

When the Germans passed through the Château Pegache area, he was told he would be left behind. He was boosted into a tree. One of the SS tied his legs so that he could not get down. They gave him a sniper's rifle and told him to shoot any 'Englanders' that came his way. He then said he had fired his sniper's rifle when he saw the Canadians coming up the hill, but swore that he made certain he had aimed over their heads. He had been given strict orders that he would remain under observation. There were still some Germans on the outskirts of the Château. It never was clear as to whether **GERD** had fired the shot that killed **BILL BIRD** or whether he had been mowed down by some retreating Germans.

On close questioning by **SZUMSKI** (both were speaking a bit of English, a bit of Russian and, presumably, some Estonian), **SZUMSKI** said the sympathies of the sniper lay with the British and that he was anti-German. In fact, he offered to fight with the Canadians against the German Army.

Astounded by his story, the men of Charlie Company, who had lost **BILLY BIRD** in what they felt was a gutless manner, took a different attitude toward this Estonian. He did seem to be a likeable guy, saying that he was a farmhand. His manner seemed to prove this.

The men who had gone after the sniper were called back to the Château because the perimeter was under counterattack by the Germans. It was with some scepticism that we saw the Estonian take off his German battle smock and join one of our own rifle sections, which was heavily engaged in fighting back the counterattack. Apparently, the RWR guys needed no further convincing that the sniper had had no choice but to obey his

German masters. We attached him to **Szumski**, who seemed glad to have him as a friend.

Gerd did 'joe jobs' in our rear echelon until much later when the Canadian Provost learned of the incident. They picked him up and that's the last we saw of our sniper. We did, however, learn a lesson. Not all of the guys in the battle smocks of the SS or the regular German Wehrmacht uniforms were necessarily Germans or loyal to Hitler.

Perhaps the most interesting development was how **Gerd** fit into our company. The three platoon commanders chatted about it. We had lost, within days, the platoon officers assigned to the company. Reinforcements, particularly officer material, would apparently take a long time in coming. After their parley, **Rfn Szumski** suggested that, for the time being, **Gerd** be attached to his platoon. He was badly under strength and he had at least one Estonian who could, in the unlikely necessity, manhandle **Gerd**. **Szumski** seemed pleased with the arrangement.

Although **Gerd** did not get a chance to talk to **Bill Bird**, he and Bill would have found something in common. This might seem to be sacrilege.

No excuse could be given for the activity which ended **Billy's** life. **Gerd** had no control over his own destiny. He was used by the higher command of the German Army as another guy to fill a soldier's uniform. 'Teach him to shoot and you have a killer on your hands.' Moreover, he could have been watched by a loyal German. He would have had no way of knowing.

Were **Gerd**, and others like him, responsible for their actions? Many tales have been told of how the foreign able bodied men were driven into battle by the P38s, Lugers and Schmeissers in the hands of ardent Nazi killers who knew no mercy. They walked behind the conscripts and forced these unwilling foreigners to 'do their dirty work.'

The connection between the soldiers such as **Tony the Italian** and **Gerd the Estonian** has seldom been written about. They had been forced to kill, whether they liked it or not.

And so the circle closes. It involved the death of **Billy Bird**, one of the most likeable, highly trained NCOs in the Canadian Army. Then a word picture is given of **Tony**, the Italian soldier who had been 'captured' by the officer in the Green Howards Regiment. Next there was **HANS** – a Pole doing the dirty work for his captors. The story continues on to **GERD** who could be a controversial subject. He was fighting against the Canadian Army, but his sympathies were certainly not German.

GERD became a real help around 'B' echelon and gave me an opportunity to understand his plight. Instead of sending him back to the POW cage, he was allowed (unofficially) to remain with Charlie Company, at least for a short while.

The more information we gathered on **GERD**, the closer I could come to placing him in relationship to **BILLY BIRD**. Strange, isn't it?

BILL turned 29 the day before he was killed. **GERD** was roughly the same age. **BILLY** was what could be called a 'shade tree mechanic.' He was one of those guys who could turn his hand to anything, whether that hand bore a wrench, a rifle, an outboard motor part or the innards of the fast universal carrier.

It was a short leap of imagination to see **GERD**, hanging around a big oak tree while Billy worked on an old jalopy at his house in the north end of Winnipeg. Perhaps in the thirties, should **GERD** have a question, **BILLY** would have taken time to answer. What a tragedy when war pits these two people against each other! **BILLY** (as has been recounted herein) would be just the type to impart his knowledge, living on the outskirts of a major city – learning what kept the farmers' machinery going, but lending a hand at any 'handyman' job.

GERD – conscripted into the Russian Army – would have abhorred the fact that his German officers would have put him in a position where he had to kill **BILLY BIRD** – a chap whom he would have taken delight in knowing in peacetime.

Sgt W.E. (Billy) Bird (left) and Sgt J.W. Thomas talk over advance route with RSM J. (Mickey) Austin

Château Pegache

Before we finish with Château Pegache and the **BILL BIRD** story, here's one for the books. A story concerning the capture of Château Pegache. One of the very able non-commissioned officers was leading a platoon. Their officer, **KEITH FURRY**, who came from Hamilton, Ontario, had been killed.

After we felt that we had the Château safely in our hands, the situation was reported to the CO. The message was sent 'in the clear.' Despite the still dangerous environment, the CO promptly bawled me out. This would have given any alert German officer the capability of breaking our unit code for at least that day. (It was changed every 24 hours.)

SGT KEN REDSHAW, who took over when **KEITH FURRY** was killed, set up some Bren guns on the ground floor of the Château. Then a noise from below. Someone was in the basement. It might have been a civilian… it might have been a German.

This called for an investigation. **REDSHAW** literally flew down the basement steps. Then he let out a yell, asking for a weapon.

He was confident that there were no longer any Germans around. He forgot his rifle. I threw him my Sten gun. Seasoned troops of the Normandy regiments will guess what happened next. The Sten gun – known <u>un</u>affectionately as the plumber's nightmare – went off and both **REDSHAW** and the German prisoners did a pretty good imitation of an Irish jig.

Unabashedly, **REDSHAW** mounted the steps holding the handle and business end of the Sten gun. Two Germans were his prisoners. The whole story was good for a laugh then. It still is.

Some people are of the opinion that the battles in the rough terrain from Caen to Calais, via Falaise, was largely a matter of slugging it out with an army composed of Germans. In actuality, many were foreign nationals, forced to wear German uniforms.

KEN REDSHAW, thorough as he was, still missed one prisoner in the darkened basement. Later I heard a mournful singing. I went down and there was a Czech prisoner forced to fight for the German army. He was singing the Czech National Anthem. I copied down the words but did not know until many years later when I read a book by **JOE SCHLESINGER**, CBC Foreign Correspondent, what the words meant. They are repeated here as they indicate the plight of those from other countries who were forced to fight for the Germans. If the printing in my diary is correct, they read as follows:

KDE DOMOV MUJ . . . KDE DOMOV MUJ?

Schlesinger's translation was:

"Where is my home, where is my home?"

Chapter 41

THE CANADIAN ARMY

I think of a hero as someone who understands
the degree of responsibility that comes with his freedom.

Bob Dylan

> To understand fully the makeup of the Canadian Army troops, there are four elements:
>
> - The private soldiers, called riflemen or ORS;
> - The non-commissioned officers (corporals / sergeants / sergeant majors);
> - The junior officers (lieutenants);
> - The field grade officers (majors / lieutenant colonels / colonels and above).

When it comes to the infantry, the four elements are engaged.

The guys that caught the imagination and did much of the dangerous work of the Infantry were the bare-knuckled, tough infantry <u>Privates</u> (ORs). The basic pay of the buck private was $1.30 ($1.10 to start) a day which is hard to imagine in today's economy.

In the early years of WWII, Canada wondered how our young men – our citizen soldiers – would stand against the arrogant killers of the Third Reich. The enemy forces viewed Canadians as the product of a degenerate society. Even die-hard supporters were not convinced that our younger generation were equal to the task. How that perception changed! Beneath that soft, easy-going, pleasant veneer were Canadians who were 'tough as nails.' My old clippings use adjectives like indomitable, tenacious, resilient. **GEN KURT MEYER** called them 'little fish.' He had plenty of reason to change his tune when he surrendered, wearing the tattered uniform of a non-descript Wehrmacht soldier hiding in a filthy chicken coop eight weeks after D-Day.

As a Canadian Army, we advanced through the hayfields of Normandy in the heat of summer. The ordinary private took it on the chin, so to speak. How can we, who survived, ever forget the khaki battledress-clad soldiers lying face down – having voluntarily given their lives and their futures in the cause of decency – to say nothing of the lifetime of suffering for their loved ones.

No description can do justice to the job which the Canadian Private (called ORs – short form for 'other ranks') did. They were, for the most part, untrained – compared to the battle-hardened Germans. Many of **HITLER'S** men had been exposed to combat on the forefronts of the battlefields of the desert or had fought it out against the merciless unyielding soldiers of the Russians – The Red Army. Fighting in atrocious conditions across the steppes of the frozen fields in that desolate country was a bitter training ground for the Germans. They had every reason to feel superior to our ill-equipped, unprepared infantry.

German troops, schooled in the battlefields of Russia or hardened in the other crucibles of war, seemed to have all the advantages.

Nothing is said of the German's iron discipline and their steely acceptance of the hardships of war. The Germans undoubtedly had an army which the world felt were the best. Then they reinforced their ranks with captured soldiers of other nationalities.

These subjugated conscripts were refused the ordinary courtesies of Germans and were called the *untermenchen* – translation – 'little more than slaves' forced to fight for the Fatherland – **HITLER'S** Germany.

Against them, the fine young boys of the Canadian Army were seemingly outclassed. Today, wandering through the fields of Normandy, the thought occurs – 'how did our Canadian boys ever make it?'

The enemy were merciless troops who had been at war for four years. Many transferred from the brutality of the Russian campaign to the easier realities of Normandy. This then is the backdrop of what lay ahead after the invasion phase. Often we fail to see the true picture of what our boys from the farms, mines and cities of Canada were up against.

This is not to say that the German Army in Normandy was a 'pushover.' The Panzer divisions, in particular, were superb fighters. Even the 'white bread' division, composed of soldiers with serious stomach problems (thus the name), was well trained. Gastric problems did not seem to hinder their ability to kill.

The German army conscripts (both regulars and SS) had superior weaponry, and their leaders were ardent Nazis. The German Army had its share of men of different nationalities. They loathed their German masters. To refuse to fight in a German uniform, however, was to court certain death for themselves and their families who continued to live in German-occupied countries. Desertion was a risky option – an immediate death warrant. So, reluctant or not, they could and did kill many Canadian soldiers.

Chapter 42

THE MÉTIS

*Of suns unwearied; all unwithered, wearing
thy valour stainless in our heart of hearts.*

Duncan Campbell Scott

The RWR could boast of 102 Métis among its ranks. These men were the direct descendants of the soldiers who fought under **GABRIEL DUMONT**, the 'battle adjutant' of the Métis in the North West Rebellion. **DUMONT** was the 'number two' man to Louis Riel.

The contribution of the Métis to the fighting troops of the RWR is described in the Regiment's history and elsewhere. How good were they? It is said, with some truth, that they could bring down an enemy or a buffalo while riding full tilt. Their tactics had been bred into them.

They were superb fighting men. Their inborn skills produced in them a superb sense of fieldcraft. Also, the Métis were skilled at the tactics of the battlefront. For centuries they had been taught how to fight. Their leaders, with their coloured feather lances, could produce a sizeable force of fighting men, emerging seemingly from behind bushes or rising out of mist-covered fields. It is well known, from reading the history of the German Army, that a sudden appearance of Métis soldiers on a hitherto unknown battleground created an aura of mystery.

It is more than a coincidence that there were three members of the **CHOQUETTE** family who died while serving in the RWR. The three **CHOQUETTE** boys were known to me. They were:

RFN MORRIS J. CHOQUETTE of Oakville, Manitoba: He died on June 8 '44 at the age of 24 and is buried at Beny-sur-Mer Canadian War Cemetery. He was the son of David and Mary Choquette. *Choquette Bay* (64 P/4) in Oolduywas Lake was named after him. It is in the same square mile as *Choquette Lake*, named for **EDMOND CHOQUETTE** (chronicled later); that is near Nueltin Lake.

RFN ROLAND J. CHOQUETTE of St. Boniface, Manitoba: He died on August 15 '44 at the age of 22. He is buried in Bretteville-sur-Laize Cemetery. He was the son of George and Aurora Choquette. *Choquette Point* (64 I/13) on Shethanei Lake was named after him. It is also in the square mile numbered 64.

RFN ED CHOQUETTE of Glenora, Manitoba: *Choquette Lake* (64 N/6) carries his name; it is southwest of Nueltin Lake. He is buried in Adegem Cemetery. He lasted longer than the other two **CHOQUETTES**, having died of wounds on October 28 '44 after a valiant battle at the Leopold Canal. He was 26 years old. Carrying on the tradition of the Choquettes, another cousin, **PTE LAWRENCE CHOQUETTE** served in the Queen's Own Cameron Highlanders of Winnipeg and died on August 8 '44.

The documentary *Against All Odds*, which I produced in 1988, contains a short vignette. I was filming grave sites, identifying the headstones of Winnipeg Rifles. I pointed to the headstones of 12 of my Company, then came to the last headstone. I was shocked and said on tape: "My God, **EDMUND CHOQUETTE**." Unbeknownst to me a German shell had killed him outright. My nerves were in tatters for several days after seeing **ED'S** grave.

WORTHY OF NOTE! It was common, prior to World War II, to call the Métis 'half-breeds.' The designation 'half-breed' fell into disuse when the RWR realized that it was a derogatory term. The descendants of those fighters who had given such a stirring account of themselves against the 'whites' from the prairies in the Riel Rebellion of 1885 deserved a better nomenclature than the ignoble 'half-breed.' They were soon assimilated into the Winnipegs and certainly achieved equal status. More to the point, those known as 'half-breeds' would resort to fist scuffs if challenged by this degrading term. The name was first shortened to 'breed' and, before the Normandy campaign finished, they were 'Métis' – the proud descendants of a fighting tradition.

The term 'half-breed' was applied primarily to those of French and Indian extraction. Where parentage was Scotch and Indian, the descendents were never given this crass name of 'half-breed.' Incidentally, the word Métis is from the French language meaning 'one of mixed blood.'

The manner in which the Métis could carry out a patrol left the regular Germans in awe and fearful. As well, mentioned herein, is their ability as snipers and marksmen.

The Métis had little opportunity before World War II to share in Canadian society. They lived in roving bands in the late 1800s. The government recognized that the Métis had some claim – probably under the 'squatter's rights' concept. Accordingly, the Métis were offered 'scrip' – little more than a piece of paper which entitled them to 200 acres. The government had announced, well in advance, that the scrip would be issued for various locations throughout Western Canada. The money-grubbing land speculators were on hand when the scrip was distributed. The Métis had no perception of the value of their land. Many instances are on record where unscrupulous entrepreneurs offered a Métis a horse or some other eye-catching article, in turn for their scrip. Those Métis who actually used the land bought with the scrip are few and far between.

Their experience in the Armed Forces in World War II should have changed the public's view of what they still termed the half-breed. Unfortunately, the Métis could not take advantage of the generous rehabilitation plans offered to returning veterans. If they wanted to enter trade school, they would need some basic education – a component which was denied them due to their nomadic existence and lack of schools. In one now-famous anecdote, a Métis with what would amount to a grade three education, gained in four different schools as his family moved around the prairies, visited a Veterans Affairs office. The counsellor ran through the options available under the Veterans Charter. The interview ended by asking the Métis if he would like to become a lawyer or a doctor – this, to a man who had no education! He had fought valiantly for his country and was among the top soldiers in the infantry. Like most of his compatriots, he walked out of the DVA office in disgust – back to a canvas and two-by-four tent on a road allowance near St. Ambrois, just north of Portage la Prairie in the Brandon, Manitoba district.

As this memoir is being written, The War Amputations of Canada is preparing to take the case of the Métis before the Human Rights Commission in Geneva. Our claim is based on the obvious fact that the returning Métis could not qualify for the esoteric career paths offered to their white brethren. To accept such offers, the veteran would require at least a working knowledge of what we sometimes call the three R's – reading, writing, and 'rithmetic. Most could not qualify.

The RWR had a good number of status Indians among their ranks. They were recruited from the reserves. They also got a lousy deal after the war, as they were unable to take advantage of the Veterans Land Act, under which they could have purchased their own land. The government's answer was that the land belonged to the Crown. This issue is still before the Human Rights Committee.

Chapter 43

COURAGE TO FACE WAR'S AFTERMATH
RFN. HAROLD PROUT

If it be found when the battle clears,
there Death has set me free,
Then how shall I live with myself through the years
which they have bought for me?

Rudyard Kipling, from *The Question*
Published after the death of his only son in World War I

Almost every soldier has a tale to tell. This concerns one who survived but with life-long damage to his face. It tells the way in which an ordinary soldier handled serious war disabilities when he returned to civil life. It is appropriate to insert this story here: first, for the sake of interest; and second, because it had its beginning while the RWR were in Shilo.

It had been my good fortune to meet **HAROLD PROUT** shortly after he enlisted. We found ourselves sitting on a bench in Brandon, Manitoba, waiting for transport to get back to Camp Shilo. There happened to be a panhandler going by our bench. The derelict took off his cap and asked for a donation. **HAROLD**, quick on the uptake, told him: "We're working this side of the street; go stake out the exit door of that pub across the way."

The laughter was loud and long, but the thought was serious. **HAROLD**, ever the wit, said within earshot of half a dozen 'Shilo-ites,' that he would get a tin cup and sell pencils if he did not get out of the war in one piece.

HAROLD PROUT is a prime example of the kind of men we had in the RWR. During battles in the Rhineland forests of Germany late in the war, he was riding in his carrier when a German airburst exploded above him. He sustained damage of the worst kind. The most devastating injury resulted from a large fragment which tore off his entire lower jaw. The gaping hole could not be repaired.

War wounds are often the acid test to determine whether the soldier did his part in combat. Was he able to handle serious medical war-caused problems when he returned to civil life? Let's see!

HAROLD was in my platoon. We still correspond on a regular basis. He was unable to return to Winnipeg – his home before enlistment. This was due to the severity of the shell wound and as he states: "The only two medical facilities in Canada at that time [1944] that could attempt to handle my facial damage were in Toronto and Montreal."

After returning to Canada, HAROLD underwent something like 25 different surgeries. The best that the medics could do was give him a supply of bandages to hide his wound and a syringe to get liquid food down his gullet. His post-war job was in the artificial limb shop at Toronto's Sunnybrook Hospital – a place I often visited on business. This gave me a chance to ask him whether the wages paid by Veterans Affairs were somewhat better than a tin cup and pencils (our private joke!). He proudly showed me his wedding invitation along with the deed to his new house. It was a heartening experience for me. HAROLD, notwithstanding the loss of his jaw, could still get a great smile with his eyes.

HAROLD PROUT, while in the UK before the cross-channel invasion, with his keen eyesight and prodigious memory, was sent to the British Army training school for aircraft identification. His expertise was essential. A signal could be sent to our own aircraft or artillery telling them 'friend or foe.'

HAROLD saw plenty of action from D-Day on, lasting through to the severe battles until a month before the armistice in May '45. His background as a homesteader meant he would be able to handle tough jobs and would seldom, if ever, need direction. In fact, HAROLD is an outstanding example of one of the basic principles of the Canadian soldier – that is, the ability to act independently should the need arise.

Is it possible to measure the courage of a man if an examination is made of the manner in which he handles the damage inflicted upon his mind or body by war? The experience of HAROLD PROUT seems to define the kind of riflemen we had in Northwest Europe. They need not take a backseat to any of HITLER'S supermen.

HAROLD had what would be a normal upbringing for Canadians joining the Forces. He was born in Portage la Prairie, Manitoba, but was raised on a homestead in Hudson Bay Junction. This is where the CN train leaves the main line for the Northern Port of Churchill. The real danger in working a homestead in that part of the world came in the swarms of mosquitoes. Also, the rail line was given to cave-ins. Riders were routinely asked to walk either in front or behind the train in case the entire embankment hit a sinkhole. This was muskeg country. The whole train could disappear. HAROLD'S job (part-time) was to walk the rail line.

So the picture becomes clear. He worked on a homestead in the mosquito-infested bog around Hudson Bay Junction. Then his family moved to Winnipeg and he went to school in that city. Next, he joined the Army where his keen sense of humour made him popular with his bunkmates.

He would need every ounce of courage when we speak of his war wound. HAROLD and I keep in touch. He will not mind if I stress the fact that he has lived for 60 years with only one-half of his face. This means that he suffers the consequences of Winnipeg weather – hot in summer, cold and dangerous in winter. His mark of distinction? His dignity was not impaired by the visual effect his facial damage had on others.

To my knowledge he has never complained, although he did ask what would happen to his wife of more than 50 years if he had to go into a Veterans long-term care facility. There is a commitment on his file now. So long as his wife has sufficient medical deterioration to warrant admission, she and HAROLD could, if necessary, move together to an institution which has been financed entirely by the generous people of this land.

Every now and again I will ask for upgrades on HAROLD'S disability. Thus far he has refused any additional pension, despite the fact that, in addition to having half his face shot away, he has a cardiac problem. Again a measure of the man.

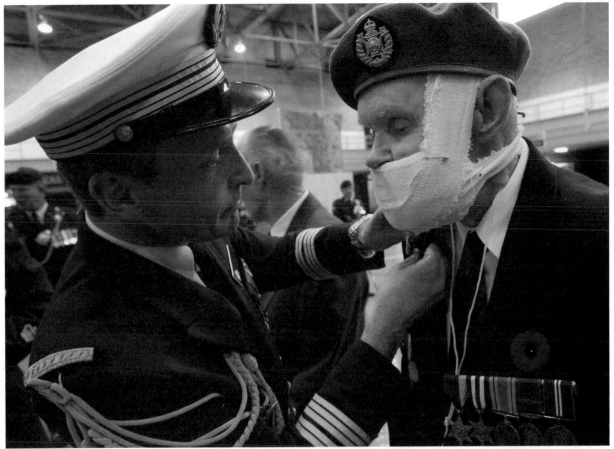

Naval Captain Olivier Casenave-Pere pins Carpiquet Medal on veteran
Harold Prout during ceremony at Minto Armoury. Prout received a
severe jaw injury during the Second World War - - November 2004

Chapter 44

ODYSSEY

The unexamined life is not worth living for man.

Socrates

Reading a book should entail a little more than stretching out on a chaise lounge in comfort. At least not this book! So . . . the suggestion is to get a good map of Normandy, the French Channel Coast and Belgium. Also a good Manitoba map.

BILLY BIRD – Felled By The Fickle Finger Of Fate

One might ask – is there any compensating factor when a visit is made to *Bird Island* (64 H/6) which the Manitoba Government has named in honour of this great soldier? The tendency is to be positive. When memory, however, brings back the incident which despoiled this beautiful laneway in France – and *Bird Island* in Northern Manitoba, which now stands as a shrine for the BIRD family – it is an easy task to come up with a rationale.

It was good fortune that placed me near the Château Pegache near Calais when I was doing a documentary on the battle for the Leopold Canal in 1994. That gave me a 'start' point.

The trip to Château Pegache had already been planned when the Manitoba Government informed me of the naming of *Bird Island*. I went north of Winnipeg in an RCAF Aircraft to locate *Bird Island*.

Pictures of the laneway near Château Pegache were close in my mind. It seemed only days later that I was paddling a canoe to *Bird Island*. No commemorative plaque was visible, although it is possible that one is there now. I was more interested in making the jump in time and space, from Château Pegache in France, where BILLY had met his end, to *Bird Island* in Manitoba, which will commemorate his valiant deeds for all time.

I imagined him, with that big moonbeam smile on his face, when he realized that **CAPT CLIFF CHADDERTON**, still with his feet planted on terra firma, was telling him what had happened ... explaining that he had been shot, not by a German, but by an Estonian forced into German uniform ... telling him that his sacrifice in World War II would always be marked by the naming of *Bird Island* ... telling him that in August '98, his wonderful wife Catherine and daughter had thought enough of him to visit Ottawa, see me and once again (with gritted teeth) hear how he had died in the defence of his country.

BILLY BIRD had married a beautiful English girl, Catherine. Together they had a daughter. He was never to see his lovely little girl grow up. Yet Catherine Bird remained very close, in her thoughts, to **BILLY**. This is borne out dramatically when she and her daughter, in January of 1945, made their trip to live in Canada. She still had the letter I had written to her after Billy was killed. This is the standard procedure and is carried out religiously in the Canadian Army so that an officer or NCO considers it a sacred duty to write to the next of kin and tell them how bravely the soldier had died.

Somehow I had the idea that rehashing **BILLY BIRD'S** death and my visit to *Bird Island* could be used to talk to his widow Catherine – and perhaps BRING CLOSURE FOR HER.

Then ... a bolt from the blue. It hit me. Catherine had no intention of dealing with closure. **BILLY BIRD** was her husband. She remembered him as a wonderful guy and the father of her intelligent, beautiful daughter.

```
I wake each morning and I promise to laugh
I look each morning at your old photograph
And I kiss you, my dear
Just as though you were here

As evening shadows start to lengthen the dark
I take the same old stroll we took through the park
And I kiss you, my dear
Just as though you were here

Now don't be afraid that distance and time
Will finally tear us apart
The further you go and the longer you stay
The deeper you grow in my heart
```

And then each night before I wander to sleep
I bring to light the dreams I cherish so deep
And I kiss you, my dear
Just as though you were here

Cliff Chadderton
The Western Front Documentary
Produced by The War Amputations of Canada

What thoughts went through my mind? IT WAS ME WHO WAS SEARCHING FOR CLOSURE. I had never gotten over the loss of the lives of so many of my friends in the Royal Winnipeg Rifles, including **BILL BIRD**. Subconsciously, perhaps, my visit to *Bird Island* would at last BRING CLOSURE TO ME. Selfish? Yes indeed, but a greater tribute to **BILL BIRD** could never be imagined.

The only spectator on my trip to *Bird Island* was **HARRIS ABATTOIR**. Harris who? Let me explain. Back in 1940, when the orderly room was being manned and recruits were joining up, some of the underprivileged did not have a name. This great-looking Métis appeared before me, brandishing a slab of cardboard off a packing crate. I asked him his name. He pointed to the words '**HARRIS ABATTOIR**.' He could neither read nor write. **HARRIS ABATTOIR** is a well-known meat packing plant in Winnipeg. He had adopted the name, although he was given a more regular name for military records.

The local clergy in a settlement near Churchill, Manitoba, had located **HARRIS ABATTOIR**. He still occasionally went by that name. He arranged for the horse, buggy and canoe. One of the more ingenious little tricks was that he had an RCMP tent he had 'cabbaged' somewhere. He had decorated it with the name and logo of the RCMP. No one went near that tent when we were seeking out the sacred ground of *Bird Island*!

Here is an interesting task. Get a cartographer's map of northern France. It might require a magnifying glass, but just southwest of the port of Calais it is possible to locate a settlement identified as Château Pegache. Put down the French map and study the one of northern Manitoba.

Find Northern Indian Lake near the border that runs between Manitoba and Nunavut. It is possible to find a place so beautiful that only Heaven could have created it.

I made the trip to the settlement just West of Churchill. Part of the trip was by *democrat* (that is, an old-fashioned buggy) and a more slightly-worse-for-wear but willing old chestnut mare, and part was by canoe.

Why take the trip? The lake is named after **CSM WILLIAM E. BIRD**, H 40503. He was the third person to enlist in the Regiment in World War II.

One would have to search in all the great infantry companies in the world to find a better soldier than **BILLY BIRD**. **BILLY**, who came from East Kildonan, Manitoba, was among the best of the ground troops who were involved in the major engagement of Normandy.

Webster's Dictionary describes a pilgrimage thusly: *"1 : a journey of a pilgrim; esp : one to a shrine or a sacred place."* When it was found that *Bird Island* in Northern Indian Lake was named in commemoration of the supreme sacrifice paid by **BILLY BIRD**, some old maps helped me track down grid 64/87.

It was pure coincidence but during a canoe trip before the war, I had paddled at the high water mark near Indian Lake. I became familiar with some of the trappers in the region. My visit to that part of the world prior to the war was to do an article for the *Winnipeg Free Press* on the coureurs du bois routes of the old North West Trading Company.

It was always in the back of my mind to look up *Bird Island*. The pilgrimage to Northern Indian Lake seemed a possibility. The opportunity of failure was scary though, so it was my secret.

My 3800-mile Odyssey pilgrimage from France to Manitoba made one point abundantly clear. When the warlords who reside in some other place decide to unleash their mad dogs, they fail miserably to respect the beauties of this planet, which they may someday destroy.

I saw the very place that **BILLY** was killed in France and, in fact, helped bury him near the Château Pegache. When a soldier is killed, an initial grave is dug and marked. The battlefield was marked with shell holes. A rifle and helmet indicating a dead Canadian lay near by. Later, the body is moved by the Graves Registration Unit to a permanent location. Today **BILL BIRD** lies in the beautiful Adegem Canadian Military Cemetery, just south of the Leopold Canal area. I felt that, if I could visit *Bird Island*, it would bring some type of closure to my own angry thoughts which assail me every now and again when I think of how a war will rob us of our best men.

As **HARRIS** and I tramped every inch of *Bird Island*, I found my thoughts transcending the world that we know. I am not an overly religious person, but I did, however, find myself talking to **BILL** who, of course, resides in Heaven.

The spiritual Odyssey from Château Pegache, near Calais in France, to *Bird Island*, near the border of Manitoba and Nunavut in the northern part of our great province, gave me a feeling of peace about which I had not been able to deal for more than sixty years.

THE CLOSURE WAS FOR ME!!

APPENDIX 'A'

EXCERPTS FROM DIARY OF

CAPT. H.C. CHADDERTON, ROYAL WINNIPEG RIFLES

My pre-War II occupation was as a news editor with The Canadian Press in Winnipeg. A diary was a 'must,' particularly during combat. The entries were made when we were in a quiet location. Most deal with specific actions in which I took part. The narrative describes various events, not necessarily in sequence. Where appropriate, reference is made to the diary. My narrative will give a better understanding of what took place.

Juno Beach. Met carrier platoon of Royal Winnipegs under Major Brian Robertson. He informed me that he had been promoted to CO Support Company and that I was to take over the carrier platoon. At approximately the same map reference I married up with Rure Fultz. Confusion prevents specific details. Ordered to take section of carriers east along the beach and report on the status of our B Company assault on the huge casement located there.

Reached casement. Had been captured by B Company, RWR. Many casualties dead or dying. An assault platoon from the combat engineers was placing an HE charge at the North West entrance of the casement. This was blown during my presence.

Reported by RT. Was instructed to take road inland through Graye-sur-Mer (approximately five miles). During day, was following various RWR platoons towards Creully where RWR were dug in on the north side of the Creully River.

D Company captured a bridge which was holding up our advance.

Was informed that bridge had been taken (Lt Jack Mitchell, Platoon in D Company).

Accompanying foot troops advance towards Putot-en-Bessin. RWRs dug in defensive positions north of the Caen-Bayeux railroad. Instructed to contact the scout cars of the Inns of Court Regiment which was in a flanking position for the British Division Careen Howards. Contact was made.

Mobile-tracked tank vehicles from the Germans attack the bridge at Putot. They turned eastward and surrounded B and D Companies of the RWR who were taken prisoner. The German eastward attack repelled by Dog Company.

RWR had been ordered to make way in a scattered manner to allow for a counterattack on Putot by the Can Scots.

Occupied position between Can Scots and Reginas. Regina Regiment had been dug in at Bretteville. Heard they had turned back 12th SS attack by tanks.

NOTE: Remainder of diary reports on patrolling, counterattacks and "stitching up" of communications between RWR units and subunits.

Detailed to take carriers along north edge of Carpiquet airfield and harbour in orchard at Marcelet. RWR and tanks of Fort Garry Horse attacked sometime July 4. I was on foot with the carrier platoon guarding the access road to the airport when a sniper bullet hit my right hand and knocked my rifle free.

Treated by Dr. Bob Caldwell at RWR RAP. Was tagged for evacuation but asked to return to the company after hand wound was dressed. The MO said okay! Safer than going to another Regiment, which was the 'drill' if wounded.

Detailed to take carriers along north edge of Carpiquet airfield and harbour in orchard at Marcelet. RWR and tanks of Fort Garry Horse attacked sometime July 4. I was on foot with the carrier platoon guarding the access road to the airport when a sniper bullet hit my right hand and knocked my rifle free.

AUTHOR'S NOTE

About the Author . . .

CLIFF CHADDERTON can lay claim to have personally known a great many of the Royal Winnipeg Rifles. As a Winnipeg Journalist and junior hockey 'all star', he was well known in Winnipeg – his hometown.

He became an officer with the militia battalion. When mobilization came in June of 1940, he went 'active' with the RWR. His first job was registering recruits. He was in charge of the main orderly room in downtown Winnipeg.

He reverted from Lieutenant to NCO and served for two years as a 'ranker.' This gave him an opportunity to know many of the other ranks of the battalion on a first-name basis.

When promoted, he formed a close relationship with the NCOs of the battalion, learning much about their family backgrounds.

He was the first NCO of the RWR to receive a field commission. He was thus a member of the officers' mess.

In Normandy he commanded the carrier platoon as a Lieutenant. Later he served as Second-in-Command of Dog Company and, when finally wounded, was officer commanding (OC) Charlie Company with the rank of Acting Major.

He was four months in combat in France and Belgium. This provided the opportunity to further develop relations with the officers, NCOs and private soldiers.

His knowledge of the personnel of his Regiment prompted him to work into his memoirs the history of those who gained recognition for their courage and/or became 'fixtures' in the battalion. He possessed a gold mine of facts. He was able to tell the story of these men in action, with background information on their lives before enlistment and as combatants with the Regiment. This memoir is a unique form of history.

NB: His friends who read the manuscript insist that his biosketch be published. It follows:

AWARDS AND ACHIEVEMENTS

❖ Knight, Order of the Legion of Honour of France (2004)
❖ Gold Cross, The Polish Combatants' Association in Canada (2003)
❖ Ontario Senior Achievement Award (2001)
❖ Commander, Military and Hospitaller Order of Saint Lazarus of Jerusalem (2001)
❖ Distinguished Canadian Award (2001)
❖ Doctor of Laws (honoris causa), University of Victoria (1999)
❖ Terry Fox Hall of Fame Induction (1999)
❖ Companion, Order of Canada (1999)
❖ Patron, Conference of Defence Associations Institute (1996)
❖ Patron, Friends of the Canadian War Museum (1995)
❖ Officer, National Order of Merit of France (1995)
❖ Erasmus Medal, Kingdom of the Netherlands (liberation of Holland) (1995)
❖ Director, Battle of Normandy Foundation (1992)
❖ Doctor of Laws (honoris causa), University of Winnipeg (1992)
❖ Honorary Member, Hong Kong Veterans Association (1992)
❖ Inclusion in CANADIAN WHO'S WHO and WHO'S WHO IN CANADIAN BUSINESS (1992)
❖ Pinnacle Award, Canadian Society of Association Executives (CSAE) (1991)
❖ Order of Ontario (1991)
❖ Officer Brother, Order of St. John (since 1990)
❖ Doctor of Civil Law (honoris causa), Acadia University (1990)
❖ Medal of Honour, Canadian Medical Association (1990)
❖ Community Action Award of Ontario (1989)
❖ Royal Bank Award for Canadian Achievement (1988)
❖ Chairman, The International Committee of Prisoner of War Organizations (since 1987)
❖ Serving Brother, Order of St. John (1987)
❖ Founder and Chairman, The War Amps Thalidomide Task Force (1987)
❖ Officer, Order of Canada (1986) (member since 1977)
❖ Knight of Malta, Sovereign Military Order of St. John of Jerusalem, Knights of Malta (since 1986)
❖ Keith Armstrong Award, Canadian Rehabilitation Council for the Disabled (1984)
❖ Chairman, National Council of Veteran Associations (NCVA) (since 1984)
❖ Patron, Hong Kong Veterans Association (since 1984)
❖ Past Vice-President, Canadian National Society for Prosthetics and Orthotics (1981)
❖ Fellow, International Society for Prosthetics and Orthotics (since 1980)
❖ Certified Association Executive diploma, Institute of Association Executives (1976)